AFTER THE WALL

A Twentieth Century Fund Paper

AFTER THE WALL

American Policy Toward Germany

by
Elizabeth Pond

 Priority Press Publications/New York/1990

The Twentieth Century Fund is a research foundation undertaking timely analyses of economic, political, and social issues. Not-for-profit and nonpartisan, the Fund was founded in 1919 and endowed by Edward A. Filene.

Library of Congress Cataloging-in-Publication Data

Pond, Elizabeth.
    After the wall: American policy toward Germany / by Elizabeth Pond
    p. cm.

"A Twentieth Century Fund paper."
Includes index.
    1. United States—Foreign relations—Germany. 2. Germany—Foreign relations—United States. 3. United States—Foreign relations—1989- 4. Germany—Strategic aspects. I. Title.
E183.8.G3P66   1990
327.73043—dc20   90-9126
    ISBN 0-87078-323-8 : $8.95
                                                                      CIP

Foreword

The transformation taking place in the Soviet Union and Eastern Europe will command the attention of scholars for decades to come. At this time, we neither know where these changes will lead nor can begin to comprehend exactly how or why they happened. But we must try; for, in effect, we must bear witness. Some of the accounts written today will become the critical raw material for the greater understanding that will emerge with time and perspective. In this spirit, we asked Elizabeth Pond to write this paper on the unification of Germany.

Pond, a distinguished journalist who was based in Bonn for ten years and is now the James and Joan Warburg Professor of International Relations at Simmons College, was already at work for the Twentieth Century Fund on a book-length project on U.S.-West German relations. Her work, like that of others in the field, has been delayed by the quite sensible desire to await further clarification of recent events. But rather than be entirely becalmed by the rapid reshaping of European affairs, she agreed to press on with a timely and thoughtful interim report. Her account focuses on the tumultuous events of the past two years that will culminate in the reunification of Germany on October 3, 1990.

Perhaps her work as a reporter has accustomed her to putting herself on the line; whatever the reasons, Pond writes with boldness, acknowledging that others working later may see things differently. For now, given the pace and significance of events in Germany, her efforts will be of immediate value, adding a richness of information and insight to the lively debate about the meaning of these changes.

At this critical juncture of history, the Fund has several books on U.S. foreign policy as well as a small number of concise reports on the changing face of Europe similar to Pond's work slated for publication in 1991. We hope that these publications will provide detail and insight to the inevitable reformulation of American policy facing policymakers, for the task ahead is anything but normal.

It is conventional to lament the constraints on national policy; but, oh, how we depend upon them. They provide form and substance for our discussions about the present and the foreseeable future. Now, at the beginning of the 1990s, we are all a bit like travelers on a suddenly frozen lake, delighted and uncertain about the prospect before us. The way forward seems freshly clear and easy, but we are hesitant, nonetheless, for who can tell if the bright new surface is firm enough to support a new direction.

Richard C. Leone, DIRECTOR
The Twentieth Century Fund
September 1990

Contents

Acknowledgment

My thanks go to David Schoenbaum for casting his gimlet eye over various versions of this study. Any questionable historical analogies I nonetheless insisted on drawing are not his fault.

Introduction

To few generations is vouchsafed the chance to reshape a world. That is today's opportunity, as the Soviet empire disintegrates, German power rises for the third time in a century, and Europe as a whole experiences a renaissance that could restore to it the dynamism of the seventeenth and eighteenth centuries.

The United States is not the same colossus now as forty years ago, when it determined the postwar order as the only nuclear power, the producer of close to half of the globe's economic output, and the only major belligerent to survive World War II essentially unscathed. But it still holds a unique position as the balancer both of East-West and West-West relations. Much will depend on its wisdom and skill in managing the present transformation.

The last time a world was shattered, it was indeed America's amateur diplomats who put it together again almost single-handedly, in what the awestruck Secretary of State Dean Acheson called "the creation." Despite abundant evidence to the contrary, they started from the novel premise that peace was not an aberration, but the norm (at least in Europe). They turned their backs on the isolationism of the 1930s and on George Washington's sage eighteenth-century (but dangerous twentieth-century) advice to avoid entangling alliances. They stationed hundreds of thousands of GIs in Europe and committed the new continent to the North Atlantic Treaty Organization—to contain the Soviet Union and to deter war altogether, so that the United States would not need to intervene a third time to rescue the old continent from its civil wars.

The Americans redressed the punitive settlement of Versailles that had so quickly led to a new bloodletting. Remarkably, they decided that the

1

way to increase their own well-being was not to hoard jealously their half of world production, but to share it in order to generate more wealth for all. In enlightened self-interest they devoted an unheard-of 3 percent of GNP and 10 percent of the federal budget to Marshall Plan aid to rebuild a war-exhausted Europe into a formidable economic rival. To that weary, cynical Europe they imparted optimism and energy as well as money. And they insisted that the Marshall Plan largess be administered not unilaterally, by atomized nations, but multilaterally by all recipients—including the erstwhile German enemy—in cooperation with one another. This requirement, along with the vision of the Robert Schumans and Jean Monnets, forged the future European Economic Community that is now heading toward the single market of 1992 and "political union" thereafter.

The Marshall Plan's help for self-help, along with the Bretton Woods invention of new international financial and trade institutions that could withstand the fatal pressures for protectionism, succeeded beyond anyone's wildest imagining. Sustained decades of economic growth followed in the West. The Federal Republic of Germany experienced an "economic miracle" that would quickly make it the globe's leading exporter. Democracy and prosperity, despite some false starts, became synonymous in the minds of West European voters and shut out the extremes of both Right and Left. And the whole structure proved sturdy and flexible enough not only to incorporate the emerging Japan into the free-trade club but also to incorporate Spain and Portugal (and an errant Greece) into the West European democratic commonwealth as they emerged from right-wing dictatorships.

At the same time, the perverse blessing of nuclear terror—brought to bear in NATO's declared readiness to resort to nuclear escalation should Western Europe ever be attacked and begin losing a conventional war—outlawed any war whatever on that parcel of earth most dear to both superpowers. Even limited "conventional" war could all too obviously slip into nuclear holocaust and could not therefore be contemplated, even by a gambler. Western Europe enjoyed its longest peace since the Middle Ages, despite the convulsions of decolonization and cold-war confrontations that included the Berlin blockade and airlift, the Cuban missile crisis, and the Berlin crisis that ended with erection of the wall in 1961.

By contrast, Eastern Europe, dominated by the Soviet army, paid the price for this precious stability; Eastern Europe was the cruel exception to the continent's "long peace," as it came to be called. In a nuclear era, prevention of war and of miscalculation was all-important; after some initial probes, the West would no more interfere militarily in the ceded Soviet sphere of control east of the Elbe River than the Soviet Union would interfere in the West. Soviet tanks ruthlessly suppressed the East Berlin workers' uprising in 1953, the Hungarian revolution in 1956, and the "Prague Spring" in 1968, and underwrote suppression of the Solidarity free trade union through martial law in Poland in 1981. The West did not lift a finger.

Indeed, by the 1980s the postwar system looked immutable. The Prague Spring demonstrated that Eastern Europe could not conduct fundamental political reform without Soviet consent. Heavy Western borrowing by Poland and Hungary in the 1970s demonstrated that half-hearted reform of command economies without fundamental political reform led to financial ruin. Martial law in Poland demonstrated to demoralized East Europeans that even if the ruling Communist parties disintegrated, the armies could step in to preserve the old stagnation. Even in the 1980s, Secretary of State Emeritus Henry Kissinger still viewed the main task of Western diplomacy as managing the rise of Russian military power and excessive self-confidence. The continued division of Germany and of Europe still seemed to be the prerequisite for stability and peace. Any East European yearnings for a better life had to be sublimated to survival.

And yet, in the end, George Kennan's containment also worked as effectively as George Marshall's economic generosity and Harry Truman's entangling alliance. Despite the fears of Western antinuclear pacifists that containment would induce war, and despite the fears of Western hawks that nuclear inhibitions would induce appeasement, both deterrence and containment proved effective. It took longer than the brief fifteen years Kennan originally envisaged. But within forty years, the West's (and Third World's) resistance to military expansion of Soviet hegemony did turn the Kremlin inward, to domestic reform. That deus ex machina, Mikhail Gorbachev, came to power in Moscow and introduced perestroika.

Gorbachev and his advisers, in varying degree, perceived a Soviet economic, technological, and political crisis and determined to rescue the system. To do so, they needed a respite from confrontation with the West and a build-down of the exorbitant arms race. They needed better quality machinery and consumer-goods imports from Eastern Europe. They became convinced, with Gorbachev's "new thinking," that the United States was not plotting an imminent attack on the Soviet Union; that in the nuclear age, guns and remote Afghan passes are less useful than butter and joint ventures; and that old-guard ideologists and rotten economies in Eastern Europe were more a burden than a gain. Progressively, they distanced themselves from the "Brezhnev doctrine" of intervening militarily in Eastern Europe to preserve ideological orthodoxy.

Increasingly, the East Europeans tested their expanding room for maneuver, until 1989 became the year of democratic (or para-democratic) revolution throughout the region. Hungary and Poland began the trend, leapfrogging each other in holding semifree elections and fully free by-elections and installing the area's first non-Communist government in decades under Solidarity Prime Minister Tadeusz Mazowiecki in Warsaw. Yet by summer of 1989, these two countries still remained the exceptions—Poland because it was big and feisty, Hungary because it was small and strategically marginal to the Soviet Union and could experiment without endangering others if its experiment failed.

And then the unthinkable happened. As the Hungarians opened their borders to the West, frustrated young East German workers began pouring over them to emigrate to the Federal Republic by the tens—eventually hundreds—of thousands. The few would-be domestic reformers in the (East) German Democratic Republic suddenly found themselves less isolated; others began joining in their demand for free elections and an end to rule by secret police. And the prize that everyone knew the Russians would never give up, the East Germany that was the outer bulwark of Moscow's western glacis, the Soviet conquest, bought with the blood of more than twenty million dead, liberated itself.

At East Germany's fortieth anniversary celebrations, Gorbachev made it clear that the Soviet legions in the GDR, in numbers more than double East Germany's own army, would not prop up septuagenarian Erich Honecker. And the East German man on the street, who since 1953 had been politically passive (and even contemptuous of the periodic Polish explosions), suddenly displayed civil courage, marched in the streets, ousted Honecker and his entire entourage, pried open the Berlin Wall, and demonstrated for German unification. Immediately thereafter, Czechoslovakia, Bulgaria, and Romania followed the German lead in deposing their old Communist leaders. Eastern Europe would no longer play victim to prolong West European peace, but would reclaim its own European heritage, civil society, and share in self-realization. Overnight, stability ceased to mean preserving Europe's and Germany's divided status quo; it required, instead, maintaining rough balance for all nations riding the whirlwind of change.

The danger is not as great now as in the late 1940s, when a savage and possibly mad czar in Moscow, a man who had murdered twenty million of his own subjects, seized a new empire of one hundred million East Europeans and acquired the atom bomb. But the far more rational Soviet Union of today still has nuclear weapons and the largest army in Europe—and its deep imperial and moral crises could still degenerate into chaos. At the same time, the newly democratic Germany, in uniting and becoming a regional superpower, is repeating an ascent that twice before in the twentieth century led to tragedy.

The outcome of these multiple transitions will depend on the Europeans' as much as on the Americans' vision and power. But the grandsons and granddaughters of Dean Acheson and Harry Truman will certainly play a crucial role in inventing the suddenly post-postwar, post-cold-war world.

The purpose of this monograph is to look at the key country in the Central European equation—Germany—and to ask what U.S. policy toward it might now produce a "second creation" that could prove as durable and wise as the first.

Chapter 1
The Wall Falls

At 7:00 p.m., Politburo member Günter Schabowski told stunned reporters that East Germans could henceforth cross the border into West Germany.

There was utter confusion as to what he actually meant. Many thought that the tens of thousands of emigrants who were deserting the (East) German Democratic Republic through the new hole in Czechoslovakia could now go directly to the Federal Republic of (West) Germany without having to take the Bohemian detour. Others surmised that the East-West German borders proper—but not the wall sealing West Berlin off from surrounding East Germany—were now open. The Politburo—or, more precisely, Schabowski and fledgling party General Secretary Egon Krenz, its only two functioning members after the GDR's paralyzed old guard had been dumped the day before—apparently intended to open both the inner-German and the Berlin crossings, but only the next day and only in controlled fashion, with stamped visas for most, but continued rejections for some.

Within minutes of the announcement, there was a popular "explosion," as one East German official described it. East Berliners, hearing the news, rushed to the exits to West Berlin that had been barred to them for twenty-eight years, and found them still barred. The crowds and the tension mounted over the next three hours. "The choice was either to let them through or shoot," explained an anxious Allied officer responsible for West Berlin security.

By 10:30 p.m., the ranking East German border guards at four crossing points in the center of the city, still lacking instructions, did the unthinkable. These servants of the most rigidly Prussian code of obedience in the entire Soviet bloc took authority into their own hands and opened the gates. The deliriously happy throngs spilled through.

It was November 9, 1989, the fifty-first anniversary of Hitler's Crystal Night rampage against the synagogues.

By 11:00 p.m., East German Interior Minister Friedrich Dickel confirmed the desperate decision of the local commanders with an official order. The dike had been breached. It was no longer possible to turn back the flood.

Champagne and tears flowed. Even the border guards were swept up in the jubilation, metamorphosed instantly from jailers to fellow celebrants. "People gave us flowers!" marveled one young recruit at Checkpoint Charlie, and regretted that his post had not been the first to wave the new tourists through. The West German Bundestag, meeting in late session in Bonn, burst into singing the national anthem, and this time, uniquely, the Greens did not walk out at such a display of national sentiment.

Throughout the night, impromptu Western hosts showered ten-mark notes and carnations and gummibears on their guests, thumped their two-stroke Trabants in welcome, and even called their nitrous plumes the perfume of freedom. Total strangers hugged each other and sang and danced on the Berlin Wall. Slight acquaintances phoned each other at two o'clock in the morning—and spent the rest of the night partying on Kurfurstendamm. Incredulous workers coming off the late shift in East Berlin strolled into West Berlin and bought bananas with their aluminum East-marks, and only afterward remembered to go home and tell their wives.

The next day, an eleven-year-old in Karl-Marx-Stadt (soon to reacquire its old name of Chemnitz, by popular referendum) rushed home from school to tell his parents the fantastic news that his teacher had said "good morning" when she entered the classroom, and the class too had responded with "good morning" (instead of the rote exchange of "Be prepared"; "Always prepared"). A nine-year-old Leipziger, asked the next week to write about the most exciting experience in his life, described the adventure as his family drove into West Germany—and the border guard smiled at them. Saturday classes were canceled for the rest of the year in the GDR, since so many pupils would otherwise be playing hooky in family excursions to West Germany.

"We found we weren't so different after all," commented one East Berlin Communist who lived two minutes away from the wall but had never before set foot in West Berlin. "What belongs together is now growing together," ex-West Berlin mayor Willy Brandt told an approving crowd of West and East Berliners in front of the Rathaus on November 10. In that one night of personal unification, Germans discovered not only that they could be as spontaneous as Latins, but also that they really were one people. West Germans, who had tended to support reunification in the abstract, while finding their poor relations something of a burden in the flesh, realized that they really did care a great deal about their brothers. East Germans, who had half feared the West's chaos and violence, were dazzled instead by the casual opulence and generosity they encountered.

*   *   *

In that one night, the postwar world of four decades vanished; 1848, 1914, and 1939, in their very different ways, were redeemed. The Right-Left schism in Germany began to heal. The Germans reclaimed their identity. The spark of revolution quickly jumped to Czechoslovakia, Bulgaria, and, more tragically, Romania, and terminated Soviet hegemony in Eastern Europe.

That wasn't the way the cold war was supposed to end, in anybody's book. Peace activists had hoped for a preliminary improvement in human nature and a rejection of those Mephistophelean nuclear weapons—and had feared that a nuclear catastrophe might first have to sober mankind into giving up enemy stereotypes. The Left had bet on Western acceptance of Communist party rule in Eastern Europe and on top-down invention there of a humane "third way" between Stalinist and capitalist exploitation that would be egalitarian, ecological, and socialist.

Western conservatives were closer to the mark in anticipating a rout of Marxism in Eastern Europe once the guns were removed and people discovered that democracy and capitalism constrain the human spirit far less than any other system. But in its heart of hearts, the Right had hardly trusted that the West's policy of containment of Soviet ambitions abroad really would turn the Kremlin inward to domestic reform. And even the diplomatic practitioners of containment, studiously avoiding "rollback" (after 1956), had worried that uncontrolled East European surges for freedom might upset stability and risk war on that part of the globe most precious to both superpowers. Gradualism was the order of the day. German division was deemed necessary for stability and peace; reunification would be possible only (if at all) at the end of a very long process of East-West rapprochement, after the opposing blocs had vanished. The GDR would be the last to free itself from Soviet tutelage.

No one imagined that the post-postwar world would be symbolized by anticlimactic *Mauerspechte* ("wallpeckers") chiseling souvenirs out of the ugliest piece of architecture in Karl Friedrich Schinkel's imposing capital.

The Chinese Wall

Until the late 1980s, it looked as if the GDR had one of the most durable—and most hard-line—regimes in the Soviet bloc. Back in 1953, the East Germans had been the first East Europeans to rebel after Stalin's death. But once the East Berlin workers' uprising was suppressed by Soviet tanks, the East Germans became more servile to their Russian masters than anyone in the bloc—as countless bitter jokes attested. They soon became the most prosperous as well—one of the witticisms observed that the drudge Germans could make any system work, even communism—and they therefore had the most to lose by agitation. East Berliners scorned the Hungarian uprising of 1956, the Prague Spring of 1968, Solidarity's strike of 1980, and the Polish and Hungarian reforms of 1989 for their romantic sacrifice of an already poor standard of living for a political will-o'-the-wisp. The East Germans congratulated themselves on their superior realism and cynicism.

Besides, everyone, East and West, took it for granted that the GDR—Moscow's high-tech supplier, westernmost outpost in the Soviet glacis, and prime trophy of the Great Patriotic War, bought with twenty-seven million Soviet lives—was the exception to Gorbachev's unprecedented permissiveness in Eastern Europe. As noted earlier, Poland could get away with experiments because it was large and feisty and had a repository of its nationhood in the Roman Catholic church. Hungary could get away with experiments because it was small and strategically marginal to the Soviet Union. The GDR, by contrast, was on the front line with the West, could hardly appeal to national sentiment without reminding its citizens of the far more successful national alternative in West Germany, and in any case was occupied by crack Soviet divisions that outnumbered the GDR's own army by more than two to one.

The very embodiment of East Germany's situation was Erich Honecker, an old Communist who had paid his dues with ten years in Nazi prisons, had supervised the overnight building of the Berlin Wall in 1961, and, since 1971, had been both party chief and head of state. In his eighteen years in power, Honecker seemed to have succeeded brilliantly in buying off and intimidating the East Germans into resignation and even a certain contentment.

The GDR's economy was clearly the most successful in the Soviet bloc. There was no (known) crisis of enormous foreign debt as in Hungary and Poland, no slipping standard of living as in reforming Hungary, no plummeting standard of living as in rebellious Poland. Bananas and kiwifruits may have been scarce, but bread and sausage were not. Random violence was far less common than in the West, child care more available. Everyone (except for the disadvantaged Dresdeners in East Germany's southeast corner) had vicarious access—via television—to Western life-styles and news; yet this access acted as opiate rather than stimulant to political unrest. East Germans occupied what was called a "niche society": parroting the required slogans at work by day, while retreating each night to their apartment niches and that fantasy world of West German television.

Moreover, the general ban on foreign travel was gradually being relaxed. In 1987, only 11,500 persons were granted a right to permanent emigration to West Germany—a figure well short of the previous three years—but 1.2 million working-age East Germans were allowed to take vacations in the West that year. In 1988, the figures grew to 29,000 granted permanent emigration to West Germany (a significant number, though still under the 1984 high of 35,000) and 1.5 million working-age allowed to vacation in the West. And in a macabre sign of progress, the automatic guns at the German-German border were being dismantled.

In addition, a certain level of dissidence was permitted. Peace activists and environmentalists could lobby for a right to conscientious objection and a cleanup of pollution, so long as they kept inside the walls of the Protestant churches that gave them sanctuary. But as soon as each new generation of ringleaders tried to carry their campaigns to the street, they were neutralized by imprisonment and/or expulsion to West Germany. For those who were agitating for permission to emigrate—a number that grew after 1984, as appetites were whetted rather than assuaged by the increased quota of approvals to leave the GDR—this was welcome punishment. For intellectuals like artist Bärbel Bohley and other moderately new-Left veterans of the antinuclear and ecological movements of the early 1980s, however, expulsion was a personal tragedy, made more bitter by popular indifference to their causes.

The GDR's internal-control system worked well, it seemed, and could perpetuate itself indefinitely. Even the advent of radical reformer Mikhail Gorbachev in the GDR's patron state failed to alter East Germany's internal stasis. Honecker calculated that a leader so alien to the Russian spirit would prove to be as transitory as Nikita Khrushchev—and that when Gorbachev was eventually replaced, the orthodox East German leaders would remain. Soviet movies and magazines that suggested otherwise were simply banned in the GDR—even if they thereby drew much more attention, as West German television reported exhaustively on the censorship.

1989

The year opened in the GDR in very nonrevolutionary fashion. Routine fraud in the spring local elections produced an official vote of 98.85 percent for the prescribed candidates. Church observers who, inexplicably, had been allowed to monitor polling places, immediately challenged the reports. Some 250 activists filed protests. They were ignored.

Even young East German proletarians, children of the system who hardly chafed at the intellectual indignities, felt no loyalty to this Germany. They were offended by having to wait twelve to fourteen years to get a Trabant, by their imprisonment inside Eastern Europe with no freedom to travel to the Alps or the Mediterranean or even next door to West Berlin until they reached retirement age. For many, the escape from boredom and regimentation lay not in reform of the recalcitrant GDR, but in flight to the much more relaxed and rich Federal Republic.

As the reform pioneer Hungary decided that its future lay in good relations with West, rather than East, Germany and opened its borders with the West in summer and fall of 1989, tens and eventually hundreds of thousands of the GDR's most productive young workers voted with their feet by moving West. Thousands of other East Germans repeatedly occupied the West German embassies in Prague and Warsaw and the mission in East Berlin, banking on embarrassing Honecker into letting them emigrate before the GDR's gala fortieth anniversary in October. The exodus threatened to cripple the GDR's industry, and did cripple the country's hospitals. For the first time, East Germany had a conspicuous economic crisis it could no longer deny.

East German officials reacted by branding those who left as riffraff and traitors—and by imposing a requirement for exit visas on East Germans visiting Czechoslovakia, the only country to which they could still travel without red tape. The government gave no sign of compromise; on the contrary, its motto seemed to be the earlier warning by Rector Otto Reinhold of the Central Committee's Academy of Social Sciences that any concession to reform would be dangerous, since it would remove East Germany's justification for a separate socialist identity and would inevitably lead to the GDR's absorption into the more dynamic Federal Republic.

Aside from the East German officials, everyone reacted to the new emigration with a surge of adrenalin. In West Germany, Chancellor Helmut Kohl and his fellow conservatives rubbed their eyes in disbelief, reveling that the reunification they had been preaching for forty years suddenly was "on the agenda." And inside East Germany, the Protestant church and the new-Left activists importuned their compatriots not to abandon the land. Bärbel Bohley, back in East Germany after a compulsory term abroad, seconded this appeal and joined with friends in mid-September to solicit more support for socialist reforms by founding New Forum, the first countrywide dissident club. The group applied for official registration as a political organization but was denied recognition and labeled "subversive" and "anti-state."

Similar proto-parties founded in the next three weeks—Democracy Now, Democratic Awakening, United Left, and the Social Democratic party—were also banned, but they pursued their political discussions regardless. And the East German Christian Democratic Union (CDU) and Liberal Democratic Party of Germany (LDPD)—two of the four "bloc parties," or satraps, the Communists had maintained as spurious proof that the GDR was a multiparty state—also began taking some initiatives of their own for the first time in four decades.

Yet emigration continued unabated; by the end of September, more than 100,000 East Germans had left.

Still, the aging and ill Honecker insisted on hailing the GDR as the best of all possible worlds on its October 7 birthday. This was a tiny affront in comparison with all of the state's more substantial infringements on its citizens' patience. But it rankled. The East Germans listened attentively as Gorbachev arrived for the festivities and made it clear that Soviet troops in the GDR would not rescue Honecker should the East German leader stumble. The decisions lay with the East German leaders, the Soviet president declared, but "life punishes him who comes too late."

For tens of thousands of East German demonstrators, Honecker was indeed too late. Over the fortieth-anniversary weekend, they took to the streets to demand reforms and shout "Gorby Gorby." Police beat them with deliberate brutality and arrested or detained some 3,500—including children and bystanders. Rumors circulated that there could be a Tiananmen-type operation in Leipzig at the regular Monday night prayer meeting and peaceful march. Secret police were primed for such an action; security forces had conducted what they called a dress rehearsal in suppressing protesters in Leipzig on October 7; extra plasma was distributed to city hospitals over the weekend; and for the first time in dealing with civil demonstrations, local military units were put on alert.

People Power

Under the circumstances, it took real civil courage for the 70,000 Leipzigers to assemble on October 9 in the country's largest demonstration since 1953 and to press for democracy and legalization of New Forum. It was less the heralding of a new era, commented one close West German observer, than "an act of despair." Yet a scant twenty minutes before the march was to begin, the police pulled back; there were no provocations by the secret police, and the event proceeded peacefully. "We are the people!" the crowd chanted.

Elsewhere in Saxony, the Dresden mayor, acting autonomously of East Berlin, met the same day with "the people," as represented by twenty of the protesters. This was the first direct contact between powerholders and dissidents, and it set a pattern. The first successful German revolution in history was bloodless.

Eight days later, Honecker's longtime heir apparent, Egon Krenz, and confederates pressed a vote in the Politburo and got the majority to force Honecker's public resignation the following day, October 18.

The sensational toppling of the undisputed East German leader of eighteen years—coming on top of the rejection of Communist tutelage in Poland and Hungary—broke the East Germans' four-decade-old habit of fear and resignation in the face of the immutable. On October 23 and 30, the crowd of demonstrators in Leipzig quadrupled again, to some 300,000. On October 26, Schabowski, acting as East Berlin party chief as well as Politburo member, met with representatives of New Forum. On October 27, the East German government announced an amnesty for those who had fled the country. On November 2, proceedings were begun in Dresden against seventy security officials for brutality against demonstrators a month earlier.

At this point, both Krenz and Schabowski were betting that they could ride the tiger. Reformed Communist parties were still assumed to offer the most feasible route to liberalization, after all, in all of Eastern Europe except for Poland, and the Solidarity government there was still thought to be something of a freak response to Poland's peculiar conditions. No one expected the Prussian Socialist Unity (Communist) party (SED) to disintegrate.

By now, however, even the cynical East Berliners decided to show that they too, like their Saxon brothers to the south, could defy authority and vent their grievances. Theater workers applied to stage a pro-democracy rally at Alexanderplatz on November 4; the new Communist leaders, for the first time, approved such a march. The police and workers' militia stood by, but did not interfere, as a crowd estimated at between 500,000 and one million turned out. East German radio and television carried the entire happening live and uncensored. "Allow New Forum," "Free elections," "Free surfing in the Baltic," and "Asterix to the Politburo" read some of the hand-painted slogans. And "No protection of the species *Wendehälse*" ("wrynecks," a kind of bird that can turn its head 360 degrees, and the instant symbol of Krenz and all the other old Communist turncoats who were suddenly presenting themselves as champions of liberalization). The crowd whistled and jeered at the two Communist functionaries who had invited themselves to speak at the gathering—Schabowski and ex-intelligence chief Markus Wolf.

"The terror regime became an encrusted bureaucracy, with no real terror. Then at some point that is the end," explained one West German Social Democrat in retrospect. "People discover that the bureaucracy can be blackmailed [in this case, by squatters in the various West German embassies]. At such a moment the emperor has no clothes. The regime becomes ridiculous," people no longer fear it, and panic sets in in the regime.

That point was reached by the eve of the Berlin rally. Less than twenty-four hours before the demonstration, Krenz, by now head of state as well as of the party, announced the resignation of five of the oldest Politburo members and sketched out an "action program" of major reforms, including an end to compulsory military training in schools, recognition of conscientious objection to military service, introduction of a public smog alarm in the worst polluted regions, institution of a constitutional court and courts for appealing administrative decisions, educational reform, and tolerance of dissidents.

On November 4 in East Berlin, unlike October 9 in Leipzig, demonstrators had the heady feeling that "people power" really counted, and that their march would help make history—East German history. Virtually none of the demonstrators interviewed by Western reporters said they wanted unification with the Federal Republic. At this point, popular awe at having shattered the old tutelage might still have given the East Germans an identity distinct from their cousins in the Federal Republic. The West Germans, after all, had not themselves wrested democracy from tyranny; they had simply been handed it at war's end, as many young West German skeptics noted. The East Germans, by contrast, were seizing democracy with their own hands.

Yet within a week it would already be too late for an independent East German course.

On November 6, the East German leadership announced a general right to travel abroad thirty days per year—but made no foreign currency available and still required bureaucratic approval that could be used to block trips arbitrarily. Throughout the country, close to 750,000 demonstrators protested this and other half measures. And the next day, even the rubber-stamp East German parliament rejected the reforms as too timid.

On November 8, the entire Politburo resigned (though key members were reappointed). Hans Modrow, the maverick party baron from Dresden, who maintained a notably modest life-style and had a reputation as a reformer, was recalled from provincial exile to join the new Politburo and was also nominated to be the new prime minister. Krenz said that there would be "free, democratic elections" and proposed separation of party and state. For his part, Schabowski told reporters that the Interior Ministry was willing to register New Forum.

Something more dramatic was needed if Krenz were to salvage the sinking morale of party and state as tens of thousands of refugees continued to abandon the GDR in that ultimate check and balance on the East German powerholders. On November 9, Schabowski, settling in as the party's rookie press spokesman, made his fateful announcement.

Democratization and Unification

The world was transformed. The dominoes of Czechoslovakia, Bulgaria, and then Romania toppled in Eastern Europe. And in the GDR, over the next month, the Leipzigers at their Monday night prayers and marches set the pace; Krenz spent the rest of each week scrambling to

catch up. On November 10, Krenz continued to introduce limited reforms, as if his whole world had not collapsed the previous night. He
yielded to protests by grass-roots Communist reformers and dropped
four of the veterans who had been renamed to the Politburo two days
earlier—though this still left eight holdovers among the thirteen full and
candidate members. And he tried to fob off the growing demand for
an emergency party congress (that could replace the Central Committee and therefore the Politburo) by scheduling only a more limited party
conference for mid-December. After further demonstrations by rank-
and-file party members, Krenz gave in and upgraded the conference to
a congress.

At the same time, the bloc parties began shedding their obeisance
to the leading role of the SED, as enshrined in Article 1 of the constitution. On November 10, the Christian Democratic Union ejected Gerald
Götting, the Communist clone who had run it for decades, and selected
as its less malleable new chairman Lothar de Maizière, an erstwhile
professional violist, a lawyer who had defended dissidents, a vice president of the Protestant Synod—and the unlikely future prime minister
of the GDR.

On November 13 and 20, despite the new distractions in West Berlin
and Göttingen, some 200,000 demonstrators showed up in Leipzig to
demand free elections and rescue of decaying buildings in the inner city,
and to place symbolic candles outside the shuttered-up Stasi headquarters. Resentment of *Bevormundung,* or being treated like kindergartners,
was so strong, and the determination to be treated like mature adults
so great, that the demonstrators could not be diverted even by the lure
of travel to the golden West.

On November 13, the Volkskammer president of thirteen years, Horst
Sindermann, resigned; the parliament promptly elected a new presidi-
um, held the first real debate in its history, and grilled government
officials—including Erich Mielke, the dread secret-police chief for thirty-
two years until his dismissal a few days earlier. Never before had the
eighty-two-year-old been obliged to report to parliament. And now the
man who had administered the whole poisonous system of internal spy-
ing automatically addressed his audience as "comrades" and could not
understand why the non-Communist delegates objected to this appella-
tion. "But I love you all!" he protested, to mocking laughter. It was indeed the melting of terror into ridicule. Within a few weeks, Mielke
and two-thirds of the old Politburo would be the subjects of prosecutors' investigations.

On November 15, the general prosecutor applied to the courts to rehabilitate Walter Janka, an old Communist convicted of crimes against the state in a bizarre show trial in 1957, four years after Stalin's death. In the next few weeks, to everyone's surprise, the once all-powerful party turned out to be an empty shell. The district first secretaries in Potsdam, Suhl, and Frankfurt on the Oder resigned or were kicked out by the local SED committees; over the next few weeks, many more party officials resigned or were forced to resign—or, in three cases, committed suicide. The minister for housing construction, some secret police generals, and trade union and other party officials also killed themselves. Hundreds of thousands of members quit the SED, and within months shrank the rolls from 2.3 million to some 700,000. The party was collapsing, everyone marveled, like a house of cards.

On November 17, a deputy from the National Democrats (a bloc party set up to attract former German soldiers) floated in the Volkskammer the idea of a German "confederation." On November 18, the Volkskammer formed a committee to investigate acts of corruption by former SED leaders, and the general prosecutor announced investigation of seventy-six cases of brutality by security forces against demonstrators on the GDR's fortieth anniversary. On the weekend of November 19, the second week after the breaching of the wall, three million East Germans visited West Germany—and returned home.

On November 20, one group of demonstrators in Leipzig sounded a new note in demanding German unification. In East Berlin, the new Politburo offered opposition groups dialogue in a roundtable that would turn into a quasi parliament before turning into a lame duck. On November 23, the East German CDU became the second party to call for a "confederation" that would reflect "the unity of the nation." Within days, "confederation" was on everyone's lips, in both East and West Germany. By November 25, Krenz himself told the *Financial Times* that he did not exclude confederation in coming years if the NATO and Warsaw Treaty alliances were dissolved. And as one East German Social Democratic party organizer observed, voters who turned out for the novel political rallies immediately asked if there would be any discussion of German unification; if not, 70 percent of them left. The Social Democrats-East were slower than their rivals to respond to electoral realities, but they too began a shift that, by the beginning of the new year, would lead to their endorsement of "the unity of the German nation" and compel the ambivalent Social Democrats-West to follow.

On November 27, a significant minority of Leipzig demonstrators waved East German flags with the GDR's emblem cut out to leave only the West German tricolor. They transmuted "We are the people" to "We are one people [or one nation]," and chanted, from the forbidden words of the GDR's anthem, "Germany united fatherland." After the fairy-tale opening of the wall and the toppling of entrenched Communist leaders in five—soon to be six—East European countries, the old innate prudence no longer set narrow bounds on popular aspirations. Unification seemed increasingly plausible. And Soviet opposition to it no longer created the taboo it would have even a month earlier.

East Germans, initially defining themselves by what they were against, increasingly realized that what they were for was what the Federal Republic already exemplified: democracy as well as prosperity. For the first time since autumn 1848, the drives for German unity and individual freedom were not in conflict. Forty years of decaying apartments, bans on holidays in the Alps, constant nagging by the state, and a standard of living only half that of West Germany had so tainted any kind of "socialism" that the man in the street increasingly echoed Konrad Adenauer's campaign slogan of "no [more] experiments" with raw, reformed, or any other kind of socialism. It was not chauvinism that drove him to display pan-German flags. It was the utilitarian reckoning that unification would be the fastest way to acquire the economic and political perquisites that West Germans naturally enjoy.

Not everyone shared this view. A number of East German intellectuals—ones who had themselves exhibited even more courage than the mass demonstrators in the years before protests became fashionable—perceived national unity as the enemy of social justice; they wanted to make the GDR a laboratory for the "true" socialism of a compassionate "third way."

Bärbel Bohley, still one of the real heroes of the whole civil rights movement, publicly charged the government with ineptness in opening the borders on November 9, before the East Germans had completed their own revolution. Her co-founders of New Forum phrased the criticism more diplomatically, but shared her basic fear that the masses, if left to their untutored devices, might expunge socialism and become "rent slaves" and the "back courtyard and source of cheap wages" to the West. They thereby relegated New Forum to irrelevance. The ordinary East German citizen rejected all socialist experiments; four months later, voters would give the new-Left slates fewer than 5 percent of their ballots.

Chapter 2
Alarums in Europe

Bonn, in the eye of the storm, was the first capital to regain its bearings. Within days of the opening of the Berlin Wall, the Federal Republic began groping its way toward resolution of the conundrum of forty years: how to let the Germans "grow together," as they manifestly wished to do, without upsetting the stability afforded by the cold-war stalemate that had given Western Europe two generations of peace—whatever the cost in division of the continent. The West, Chancellor Kohl and Foreign Minister Hans-Dietrich Genscher felt, must seize the chance for a new beginning that was arising from the conjunction of Soviet domestic preoccupation, loss of Soviet will to external empire, the bankruptcy of the Communist system throughout Eastern Europe, the determination of people emerging from four decades of repression to salvage their lives fast, and the dynamic of a newly rejuvenated European Community. In doing so, however, East and West together must find a new concept of stability that could no longer mean prolonging the vanished status quo, but would entail instead turning the force of virtually autonomous developments to constructive rather than destructive uses.

Internationally—especially in view of Germany's dark history and the latter-day economic and political well-being bestowed on the Federal Republic by interdependence with the West—the coming unification had to be embedded in continuing European integration, the West German government reasoned. Only a strong Western Europe could, in any case, remain a magnet for Eastern Europe and maintain the impetus of democratic change there. "Widening" the European Community toward the East and "deepening" it—far from being contradictory, as the French were arguing—were complementary in Bonn's view. Applying this logic,

Kohl dropped his previous resistance to France's pet European Monetary Union and a central European bank—though he did insist on German terms of bank independence and on implementation only after the West German election at the end of 1990.

In inner-German relations, Kohl's response to the gathering East German sentiment for unification—again, on grounds of stability—was countercyclical. By now, the chancellor was convinced that merger was inevitable and needed no push. He worried, however, that the number of East Germans deserting the GDR for the Federal Republic might swell to millions and incapacitate the East German economy. He worried even more that the so far heroically disciplined Leipzigers might get carried away by frustration and patriotic fervor, provoke the Soviet Union, and spark a dangerous, unpredictable confrontation. He therefore decided to apply some brakes. His aim was to give the East Germans the prospect of an orderly process toward union—via the suddenly consensual "confederation"—in order to avert any desperate calls by demonstrators for more radical measures.

To this end, Kohl made a multipurpose speech in the Bundestag on November 28. In it he sought not only to give his East German listeners enough hope to calm them, but also to give other Europeans an assurance of West German sobriety and commitment to West European integration—while at the same time, of course, assuming for himself the mantle of a twentieth-century Bismarck for the election year 1990. In ten points he proposed forming joint East-West German economic, environmental, and other commissions that could lead to "confederal structures"—an even vaguer concept than "confederation"—and then, in the unspecified future, to "state unity." As he spoke, Kohl already had East Berlin's quiet consent to form these commissions.

The Leipzigers may have been pacified by Kohl's outline, but the other Europeans most decidedly were not. The chancellor's speech was almost universally misinterpreted abroad as a deliberate acceleration rather than deceleration of events. Given twentieth-century German history, any prospect of German reunification was bound to alarm non-Germans, of course. But Kohl also exacerbated the reaction by failing to give his neighbors the kind of diplomatic briefing that normally precedes major policy statements. After the fact, the chancellor justified the lapse by saying that no one should have been surprised, since he was only replaying conventional wisdom in envisioning modest confederation.

The more pertinent reason for his secretiveness, however, was domestic—and especially coalition—politics. Up to that point, Kohl, despite the Christian Democrats' litany about German unity over the years, had not yet captured the public imagination on unification. Honorary Social Democratic party (SPD) Chairman Willy Brandt and Liberal Foreign Minister Genscher had both done much better at catching popular resonances. Kohl was determined to remedy this situation, and he did not want any premature leaks to let Brandt or media star Genscher preempt him in leading the march toward the confederation that the main German actors now agreed on.

Kohl's political management was rewarded. From November 28 on, the chancellor was the undisputed pilot of German union. Ironically, the objections of other Europeans to what they perceived as his headstrong lunge for reunification only helped establish his domestic reputation.

The Soviet Nyet

The foreign misgivings varied by nation. The Soviets, who stood to lose the most in prestige and were the most alien to the thought processes driving the Germans, were the most negative. Gorbachev had grossly underestimated the forces his permissive "new thinking" would unleash in East European countries, which already possessed, to greater or lesser degree, the civil societies and individual initiative that he was trying so desperately to graft onto the Soviet body politic. Typically, he observed to Modrow on the latter's visit to Moscow the week after Kohl's ten-point declaration, that the GDR now had cleared the way for its own perestroika. As he spoke, "citizens' committees" had already gone far beyond perestroika-type tinkering to occupy secret-police headquarters in major East German cities, and East Germany's non-Communist parties were already beginning their race to catch up with the population in calling for union with the Federal Republic.

An additional block to Gorbachev's comprehension of the dynamism of German events was psychological. After all of Gorbachev's and others' revelations about the nasty Afghan war, Soviet massacre of captive Polish officers at Katyn, Stalin's murders, and Brezhnev's stagnation, the Soviet Union had only one success it could claim from seventy miserable years: the incredible heroism with which it had endured and finally repulsed German occupation in World War II. The role of Moscow's GDR client in symbolizing this triumph was even more important than its security role as Soviet glacis. All of the Eastern superpower's nuclear might could not erase Russian awe of German military technical prowess, and all the Federal Republic's willingness to help develop the Soviet Union economically could not erase the humiliation of watching that GDR slip out of the Soviet orbit not only into neutrality but into alliance with the Western adversary.

It was hardly unexpected, then, when Soviet government spokesman Gennady Gerasimov warned, in the wake of Kohl's speech, that "it is not the time now to talk about reunification." Or when Foreign Minister Eduard Shevardnadze expressed "great concern" about the "attempt of some circles in the FRG to place the question of the reunification of Germany on the agenda." Or when Gorbachev himself declared that realities must be recognized and reunification was no issue for current policy. Or even when some Soviet commentators resuscitated briefly the old bogeyman of German "revanchism"—that is, a vengeful threat to recover former German lands awarded to Poland at the end of World War II.

West German analysts noted optimistically that while the Soviets were ruling out German merger now, they were not ruling it out in the future. The Federal Republic's allies reserved judgment.

The British and French Nyet

British officials were not as blunt as their Soviet counterparts, but their desire to see German unification postponed as long as possible was unmistakable. Prime Minister Margaret Thatcher, no friend of European integration, seized the opportunity to cite the tumultuous change and uncertainty in Germany as a reason to retard the "deepening" of political cooperation within the European Community. But otherwise she consigned German union to the distant future—after the turn of the century, when the neophyte democrats throughout Eastern Europe might have fully demonstrated their capacity to sustain pluralism. Two weeks after Kohl's address, when the Soviet Union suddenly proposed the first four-power meeting in Berlin in eighteen years, Britain and France both welcomed the opportunity to hide behind Soviet skirts in implicitly reminding the Germans that the World War II victors still held residual rights and expected to exercise them on the issue of German unification. West German media, with some bitterness, registered the intent to prolong limitations on German sovereignty forty years after the end of World War II.

France's acclimatization to the new realities was even more painful than Britain's. The French had not suffered as many deaths as the Poles or the Soviets in World War II, but they carried the resentments and fears of three German occupations and two centuries of French-German animosity. While the large majority of the French public under fifty years of age favored reunification, historical memory still preserved aversion to it among France's powerful political class. And the consternation of the elite bureaucrats was all the greater because the winds of change were sweeping away their Gaullist dreams of French rather than German leadership of Europe and their comfortable assumption that Paris could stay aloof from NATO's military command indefinitely and still enjoy the alliance's protection.

In the early 1980s, President François Mitterrand had decided that the most prudent policy would be to hug the West Germans as close as possible to avert any "drift" by them to the East. Now that the specter of unification suddenly loomed, he reacted intellectually within this special relationship by insisting to Bonn that "deepening" the European Community must take precedence over "widening" it, and on warning against letting any conflict arise between German and European union. "Widening" the European Community to take in emerging East European democracies, as West Germany increasingly wished to do, would forfeit "deepening" it politically and condemn the European Community to remaining purely economic, the French argued. They therefore pushed on an open door in the Federal Republic in nagging Bonn to support European Monetary Union and a European central bank.

Mitterrand's and France's emotional reaction was much sharper than this policy suggested, of course. The Foreign Ministry in particular—and some of Mitterrand's advisers—clung to the old suspicions of Germany. Within days of Kohl's ten points, Mitterrand, in an ostentatious snub of Bonn, told an American newspaper—before telling Kohl—that he would visit the GDR on December 20. This breach of courtesy irritated the West Germans both because it propped up the discredited Krenz, who was still in office at the time of the announcement, and because it constrained Kohl's schedule; the chancellor would eventually manage to be the first Western head of government or state to visit new Prime Minister Modrow (after Krenz's fall) only by nipping into the GDR the day before the French president. Mitterrand then compounded the affront by declining Kohl's invitation to a joint inspection of the Berlin Wall—and by flying to Kiev to see Gorbachev in early December in pointed reversion to an amoral, nineteenth-century balance-of-power feint against Germany.

Numerous West Germans read economic envy of Germany into French and British reactions, along with some nostalgia for the lost glory of empire that lingered on only in the reduced form of four-power rights in Berlin and Germany. The normally thin-skinned Kohl, for his part, said nothing publicly, but waited until such time as more Cartesian analysis might show Mitterrand that his original promotion of a French-German "alliance within the alliance" was indeed the correct course— and that there was no alternative.

The American Yes

Among Bonn's allies, adjustment to the turbulent new era was least difficult for Washington. Ahistorical America regarded flux as the norm, in any case. And for decades the distant, huge United States had felt much more relaxed about the prospect of German unity than had Britain, France, and Italy. The United States believed in self-determination, and it stood by NATO's repeated postwar pledges of support for unification, should the Germans choose this option.

Like Germany's neighbors, the United States misinterpreted Kohl's ten points as acceleration and thought the chancellor was moving too fast. It also questioned whether Kohl's failure to mention NATO in his speech might be an omen of German drift away from the West. Basically, though, Washington trusted the forty years of democracy in the Federal Republic, and, provisionally, it trusted the East German revolution.

German unification would have looked utterly different to the United States had Europe not already agreed on a single market by 1992 and, implicitly, political integration thereafter; had Gorbachev not decided to cut radically his half million troops in Eastern Europe; and had President Bush not already fixed on a strongly pro-Europe and pro-German stance at the NATO summit in May 1989. Without this combination of reduced Soviet threat and firm anchoring of Germany in Western Europe, U.S. policy conceivably might have echoed early Reagan and late Carter administration fears that Moscow might play a "German card" in offering German unity in return for German neutrality, thus "Finlandizing" Germany and driving "wedges" between the Federal Republic and its NATO allies. The administration might have gravitated to the same kind of alarm over increasing West German trade with the Soviet Union and Eastern Europe, the same anxiety that the Federal Republic might succumb to peace euphoria and cut defense budgets irresponsibly.

Under the circumstances, however, Bush and Secretary of State James

Baker stuck with their prescient decision of half a year earlier to accord Bonn the new status of America's senior European partner and to welcome West European integration fully, without the reservations of previous American administrations. In early December, with this groundwork already laid, Bush, addressing NATO members in Brussels, and Baker, addressing reporters in West Berlin, simply set forth guidelines for an eventual German merger. These included stability, consultation with allies and neighbors, respect for Soviet security needs—and yet continued membership of any united Germany in NATO. Then, in the Soviet-summoned meeting in Berlin of the four powers' ambassadors to Germany, the United States signaled that the four powers would not dictate terms of settlement to the Germans.

Influential portions of the West German media were still suspicious of American intentions. "The more Germans in both states strive for new unity," complained the weekly *Stern,* "the more unambiguously the erstwhile victors lay stones in the way—above all Soviets and Americans. In unison, they swear by 'stability.' " For *Stern,* stability still meant the status quo.

Chapter 3
Acceleration

Within the GDR, political demands for democracy—fueled both by the demonstrators' initial successes and by new revelations about the nether world of the party and secret police—suddenly became more radical in early December. Or perhaps it would be more accurate to say that, as fear ebbed and indignation grew, these demands became more specific.

The palpable fear of decades had been consciously defied by a minority of activists back in October, and had vanished for the man in the street the night of November 9. In December, the subconscious inhibitions and self-censorship on one's very thinking also faded. It was not that all risk was gone; the Stasi lived on as a kind of autonomous nervous system, and would continue to do so long after self-formed "citizens' committees" thought they had the hydra under control. But the fact that it lacked a head in the disintegrating SED leadership meant that the Stasi's mechanisms for controlling the population ceased to function. There were fewer and fewer constraints on popular anger as revelations about corruption and abuse of power in the party-state piled up in late November and early December.

Most of the corruption was rather modest; there was no Ceausescu-type megalomania, only such perquisites as villas, hunting lodges (with game all but led on a leash to where the elderly rulers could shoot it), and access through special stores to videoplayers, fresh fruit, and other delectables that any middle-class West German family could buy at will. But in a society that had boasted of its egalitarianism, the "preaching of water and swigging of wine" shocked citizens who had taken for granted the anti-Fascist virtues of the GDR and who thought that Prussian Communists were immune to the penchant of power to corrupt.

In this light, the discovery by East Germans that their leaders had been greedy made a mockery of their own sacrifice of forty years.

Two scandals in particular exercised protesters at the beginning of December—the discovery of illegal exports of weapons to the Third World by a Rostock company with shadowy ties to the old hierarchy, and the revelation that old Stasi documents, videos, and audiotapes were being destroyed.

By now Krenz and his entire team (except for the reform-minded Modrow) were utterly discredited. On December 1, the SED let the Volks-kammer repeal the constitution's guarantee of the Communists' leading role, in deliberations that lasted all of fifteen minutes. On December 3, the entire Politburo and Central Committee of the party, including Krenz, resigned. Honecker and eleven other leading personalities were expelled from the party. The former economic czar Günter Mittag and two other former high officials were arrested. An ad hoc working group was named to run the SED (contrary to all party statutes); the party congress was advanced to December 8. Citizens' committees quickly occupied local Stasi headquarters in Dresden, Erfurt, Gera, Leipzig, Suhl, and East Berlin to prevent further destruction of incriminating evidence. The top Stasi command—now called "Nasi" in a cosmetic name change that gave its acronym an unfortunate resemblance to "Nazi"—resigned December 5. The citizens' takeovers were conducted without violence, and generally by prior agreement with the regular police, who had become only too glad for the public rehabilitation that endorsement by citizens' committees offered them. But at the same time, there were (exaggerated) reports of East German civilians forcing their way into Soviet garrisons. At this point, the orderly Germans in both East and West feared anarchy and "lynch justice" in the GDR, as the rigid governing structure of four decades vanished.

In this atmosphere everyone—opposition, SED, West German officials, and both superpowers—rallied to shore up the Modrow government and prevent its collapse into potentially dangerous instability.

Church leaders had already offered to host a roundtable comprising representatives of the SED, the bloc parties, New Forum, the Social Democrats, and other groups. This new quasi parliament held its first session December 7, immediately set the country's first free election for the following May, and launched an investigation of the secret police that yielded the startling information that the Stasi had employed 85,000 persons full-time and could claim one million informers out of a population of sixteen million.

At the same time as the roundtable got under way, the SED pulled itself together at its party congress. It decided against disbandment; instead, it renamed itself the Party of Democratic Socialism (first SED-PDS, later just PDS). It swore to accept whatever minority role voters might accord it in a free election and looked to its new chairman, lawyer Gregor Gysi, to preserve the remnants of its membership.

In a bolstering of Modrow from the West, James Baker paid the first visit by an American secretary of state to the GDR (though he made it clear that the United States supported German unification). And Kohl, in his first official meeting with Modrow, in Dresden on December 19, was cordial to his host, announced additional help to East Germany of 3.5 billion deutsche marks, and went out of his way to dampen the chants for a unified Germany among demonstrators. West German President Richard von Weizsäcker gave a long television interview urging both East and West German viewers to stay calm.

By Christmas, it was clear that the East Germans would not riot: 1989 ended with a joint New Year's binge at the newly opened Brandenburg Gate in Berlin.

1990

In the new year, a certain hangover set in on all sides. The welcome dismantling of the old structures continued: On January 1, the Main Political Administration in the army ceased its functions; on January 2, the ADN news agency carried the announcement that the old Politburo villa district of Wandlitz in East Berlin would be turned into a "rehabilitation sanitorium"; and the leadership began to admit that the GDR generates some of the worst industrial pollution in the world. But now that union was virtually a given, worry began about all the conditions—the looming unemployment in East Germany's uncompetitive industries; the buying out and export by speculators of subsidized goods from the GDR; the potential reclaiming of houses and lands by West Germans who had been dispossessed of their holdings forty years before; the eventual worth of East-mark savings in "real money."

The cordiality between Kohl and Modrow also suffered strains. The Bonn coalition—which was ready to pay whatever it took to execute a new "economic miracle" in the GDR, but believed that private investment had to provide the bulk of the money—had been pleased with Modrow's promises in December about moving toward a market economy. In particular, Kohl welcomed Modrow's intention, as Bonn understood it, to allow majority foreign shares in small- and medium-sized joint ventures. But Bonn felt duped when Modrow's subsequent government declaration, on January 11, sounded, as one West German official put it, as if it could have been written by Honecker. The Kohl government, though already giving the GDR money for environmental and telecommunications projects, became chary of pouring major grants into an economy that was not liberalizing fast enough to absorb them.

For its part, the Modrow government resented Bonn's financial hesitancy. Increasingly, Modrow and the roundtable—which reflected the views of East Berlin intellectuals more than those of the general public—interpreted Bonn's stance as intervention and bribery of East German voters with promises of money only if they supported the conservatives in the forthcoming election.

Domestically, the roundtable developed its own suspicions of Modrow and the revamped PDS over two related incidents: the PDS's hyping of the threat of neo-Nazi extremism and the effort to justify perpetuation of the Stasi/Nasi. With a few exceptions, the top command of the secret police had moved over to the new Office for National Security (Nasi)—and then resigned just two days before the roundtable's first session. In January, Modrow scrapped the name "Nasi," but tried to continue the organization with yet another name change.

The roundtable would have none of this—nor would citizens throughout the country, who were fed up with being spied on. Various demonstrations and strikes over the issue peaked on January 15, in the storming of the central secret-police headquarters in East Berlin by tens of thousands of protesters. Some roundtable members, noting that the mob raced directly to the most sensitive files, saw in this uncharacteristic forced entry a provocation by Stasi operatives in a last attempt to rally the old "law and order" forces to preserve Communist power.

In the event, no forces rallied. Before Honecker's and his own fall, Erich Mielke had boasted that if any need arose, his special Stasi regiment could take control by itself. Yet his regiment and the close to one million men under arms in the country's army, border guards, secret police, regular police, and workers' militia were now paralyzed. Some senior Stasi officers committed suicide. Others, like foreign-trade czar Alexander Schalk-Golodkowski—who defected to West Germany just ahead of the East German prosecutors—expressed to debriefers their feelings of betrayal and shock that Moscow had not rescued the Honecker regime that had been so loyal to it.

In the end, Modrow avoided a major row with the roundtable only by agreeing to dismantle the Nasi and to leave establishment of any successor organization to the future elected government.

As if all this weren't bad enough news for Modrow, the GDR's increasingly available economic information now began to reveal that industry was in even worse shape than specialists had assumed, with many firms unable to pay their debts. And the paralysis of local government was becoming serious as more and more community apparatchiks resigned or were jailed, and as those who remained at their posts proved incapable, in the absence of the old centralized command, of making their own decisions. Symptomatically, East Berlin could not even manage its own garbage collection and asked the West Berlin Senate to take on the task.

Under the circumstances the hemorrhage of mass emigration continued.

Now the worry was not disorder, but collapse. At the end of January, Modrow and the roundtable advanced elections to March 18 to shorten the period of limbo, and they agreed on an emergency "government of national responsibility" that all major political groups would join.

The rapid decay in the GDR alarmed Bonn. Concluding that stagnation would be far more destabilizing than forward motion, the West German government accelerated the pace of developments, with a dramatic offer. Overriding the vociferous objections of the central bank, it proffered the GDR monetary union with the mighty deutsche mark, even before political union.

Rebuilding Consensus in West Germany

Bonn's invitation to financial and currency union worried the West German taxpayer and both comforted and worried the East German citizen who was plunging into the Western paradise and rat race much sooner than he had anticipated. This turmoil, along with gnawing uncertainty in the six weeks before the election could legitimize a new government in East Berlin, produced a surface malaise that disguised a fundamental political realignment in West Germany. Unbidden, the East German revolution and imminent German unity were prompting a rapprochement between Right and Left in the Federal Republic.

Reconciliation began with the common euphoria of November 9. The

East German revolution was greeted as the answer not only to the division of 1945, but also to the aborted revolution of 1848, to Europe's long civil war begun in 1914, and to the failure of the Germans to resist Hitler during the twelve years of the Third Reich. It was seen further as the answer to the bad conscience of the West Germans, who had been handed democracy as a gift by their Western conquerors and occupiers and had never wrested it for themselves.

Now the peaceful revolution in the GDR showed that Germans too could shed their excessive deference to authority, to act in the cause of democracy and freedom. It demonstrated that these Germans could demythologize and nullify their own authoritarianism without waiting for others to do it for them. It also reassured a self-doubting West Germany that its own values were worthy of admiration and emulation. And it gave any restless souls yearning for metaphysical identity plenty to keep them busy in the enormous task of rebuilding the East German economy and polity.

Most immediately, approaching German unity strengthened the West German center by assuring Kohl's reelection in the Federal Republic—however much this might be obscured by uneasiness before the March 18 election in the GDR. The chancellor shot up in opinion polls as the incumbent (and beneficiary of a booming economy) when the miracle occurred, and as the keeper of the grail of unification over the years.

Kohl also benefited from the (small but pivotal) Liberals' incentive to stay in coalition with the conservatives in order to share in the success of unification. Liberal allegiance was, in any case, not yet a pressing question. The German voters' preference for stability—and the backbiting within the Free Democratic (Liberal) party each time the party defected from Right to Left or back again—had established a rule of thumb for Liberal adherence to whichever coalition the party was in. A Liberal switch to the Left was therefore unlikely until the election midpoint of 1992—ten years after last jump. Still, the Free Democrats had begun to murmur about a shift in early 1989, and the prospect of German unity provided welcome insurance for Kohl that his plurality in the December 1990 election would be high enough to give the Free Democrats no mathematical choice of opting for a Center-Left government.

Unless, of course, the far-Right Rep iblicans got over the 5 percent hurdle to enter the Bundestag and deprive the moderate Right of a stable majority in the same kind of spoiler role that the Greens were playing on the Left. This threat looked serious prior to November 9. The Republicans had sprung up from nowhere to win a 7 to 8 percent anti-foreign protest vote in local and European parliamentary elections in early 1989. They were not nationalists in the old sense of seeking German subjugation of neighbors, but they were xenophobic in resenting the competition of Turks and other "guest workers" for jobs and housing within West Germany. And their bland slogan of putting German before European interests hardly veiled their chauvinist resistance to European integration.

Given the rise and precipitous fall of the far-Right National Democratic party twenty years earlier, mainstream politicians were confident that the Republicans would eventually fade away. They worried, however, about how long the decline might take; they feared that the Republicans might well peak during the December 1990 election and produce an unstable four years in the Bundestag. Yet, after November 9, the deus ex machina of approaching German unity hastened the decline of the Republicans by overwhelming their subliminal nationalist appeal. In the course of 1990, the Republicans would dwindle to below 5 percent in opinion polls and, in the process, would be rent by intramural personality feuds.

Within the political mainstream, approaching German unification began to bridge the Right-Left schism that had bedeviled West Germany to greater or lesser degree since the 1950s, when Konrad Adenauer forced his countrymen to choose the sure defense of Western alliance over the chimera of Soviet-sponsored neutral reunification. The first West German chancellor's thesis that only an unambiguous Western identity could eventually secure German unity had been mocked by Left nationalists over the years as a Rhinelander's anti-German casuistry that had forfeited unification. Social Democrats under Kurt Schumacher had deliberately seized on this issue to establish the national credentials of their party, which had repeatedly taken a drubbing for its international priorities. In the early 1950s, in the name of reunification, the SPD had bitterly fought West German rearmament and membership in NATO. Thereafter, there had always been a certain tension—sometimes tacit, sometimes explicit—between the Social Democrats' security and German policies.

To be sure, the SPD had made its peace with a West German army and Western alliance in the landmark Bad Godesberg program of 1959, which rejected dogmatic Marxism. And in the 1970s, it was conservatives much more than Social Democrats who had polarized politics by branding Social Democratic Chancellor Willy Brandt's conciliatory Ostpolitik as betrayal—until the conservatives regained the chancellory in the 1980s and themselves adopted Brandt's policy of "small steps" in dealing directly with Honecker.

But the ideological nostalgia and bitterness of the West German Left remained. The Left admired the old-fashioned, unspoiled idyll of East German villages; maintained a utopian view of the GDR's possibilities; and hoped, in common with prominent East Berlin intellectuals, for that compassionate third way. In moments of stress, the SPD longed to get back to its original pacifist ideals, even if this reversion risked shaking the domestic consensus on security and loosening Bonn's ties to the West.

In this vein, during the feud over deploying new American nuclear missiles in Germany in the early 1980s, the SPD's left wing and the Greens deplored the U.S. nuclear presence in the Federal Republic as a victimization of Germans that was little better morally than Soviet hegemony in Eastern Europe. The party opened a formal "dialogue" with the SED, as if the latter held no repressive monopoly on government but were a fellow party in a pluralist system, and signed joint appeals with the SED for various nuclear- and chemical-weapons-free zones that ran counter to Western alliance policy. Some revived the old charge that Adenauer's alliance with the West had sacrificed German unity, while neutrality might have won it from Stalin. And some came close to considering peace and continued alliance with the West as incompatible. With political attitudes among twenty- to forty-year-olds shaped during the wave of revulsion at U.S. intervention in Vietnam, this new Left frequently made blanket condemnations of the United States—in mirror image of the Reagan administration's condemnation of it—that carried overtones of German hubris in the early twentieth century about the spiritual superiority of German "culture" over Western "civilization."

Among prominent politicians, this inclination was most marked in Oskar Lafontaine, the SPD leader in the Saarland, who was being groomed in the early 1980s to become the party's chancellor candidate in 1990. At that time, while other SPD spokesmen were qualifying their opposition to NATO's new nuclear missiles by pledging continued support for the NATO alliance, Lafontaine was vigorously advocating West German withdrawal from the NATO military command, on the French model. He dropped his bid for West German aloofness from NATO only after NATO proceeded with missile stationing, Kohl won the 1983 election, Gorbachev reversed Soviet policy to agree with Reagan to scrap all Soviet as well as American intermediate-range missiles—and nuclear deployments ceased to be an acute issue in the Federal Republic.

In early fall 1989, in the opening skirmishing for the 1990 election, the SPD again began gearing up for what could have turned into a major quasi-nationalist campaign—running against limitations on German sovereignty imposed by the British, French, and, especially, American allies in low-level training flights and the damage to property during maneuvers. With the Soviet threat gone, they argued, it was insulting for the West to continue these impositions on the Federal Republic.

Paradoxically, the Left nationalist corollary in the German question turned out to be increasing SPD insistence that Bonn recognize the permanent division of Germany into two states. Egon Bahr, the architect of Ostpolitik under Willy Brandt, articulated the view that German unity could be achieved ultimately only by accepting two equally sovereign German governments for the foreseeable future—and by persuading the Soviet Union, through sweeteners if necessary, to let each of the two go its own way. In this view, the key to German unification lay in Moscow, as the shorthand phrase had it, and Moscow had to be assuaged.

Though the Greens and one portion of the Social Democratic Left criticized the SPD for ignoring the suppressed human rights of East German dissidents, the more numerous antinationalists among Left Social Democrats found this position compatible. For their part, centrist SPD leaders did not contest such an abstract policy, as everyone still deemed it, of such low salience. Upgrading East-West German representation to formal ambassadorial level and canceling the Federal Republic's offer of instant West German citizenship to any East German asking for it became SPD policy almost by default.

With November 9, however, the Left's world was shattered. Adenauer's original hypothesis was vindicated. The now risible SPD dialogue with an SED that East Germans themselves rejected gave Kohl a handy stick with which to beat his rivals. And once censorship was lifted, and the East Germans began voicing their pent-up grievances, it became clear that in the supposed idyll of the GDR a fifth of the apartments were certified uninhabitable; a fifth of its water was certified undrinkable; sulphur dioxide air pollution was quintuple West German levels; official blackmail, instead of prosecution, of criminals was routine; East Berlin's Schönefeld Airport was a center for drug running; the GDR harbored West German terrorist fugitives; and the country's main nuclear reactor near Greifswald had an alarming history of hushed-up accidents, one of which had come within a hair of meltdown.

Both main planks of the West German Left—that is, West German sovereignty in military affairs and full recognition of the GDR—were thus rendered obsolete. The first was eclipsed in the minds of voters by the much more gripping issue of unification, and was then preempted by American insistence—to the Soviet Union (as well as to Britain and France)—that the unified German state have complete sovereignty. And the bankruptcy of the SED regime left nothing to recognize and made the West German Left's romantic vision look naive. On November 28, Social Democratic spokesmen in the Bundestag could only applaud Kohl's ten points.

The pragmatic Social Democratic applauders in parliament accurately represented the basic trend of public opinion. They did not, however, represent either the Greens or one particular group of Left Social Democrats. The latter picked up the foreign criticism of Kohl's speed and lack of prior consultation on unification and, temporarily at least, reversed the SPD's approval of Kohl's position.

The SPD's own German policy, however, was in disarray. Willy Brandt, mayor of West Berlin when the wall went up, later chancellor, still later flirter with the Greens' suspicions of the West, and for years the Christian Democrats' bete noire, embraced German unity as a natural development. He became an elder statesman and even developed a certain personal closeness to Chancellor Kohl. Oskar Lafontaine, though a favorite political "grandson" of Brandt and a spokesman of the Left, took a very different tack in continuing to resist unification and appealing to discontent among West German taxpayers about having to bankroll East German immigrants now and a rise in the GDR's standard of living later. Still other Social Democrats, fearing that their party would repeat history and again alienate voters by an antinational stance, proposed even faster confederation than Kohl was advocating.

Not surprisingly, then, the totally new situation in the GDR ignited a fierce row on the Left over fundamental orientation as well as over operational policy. Even before the SPD split over Kohl's ten points, the Left leapt into polemics. West Berlin novelist Peter Schneider, writing in the Berlin countercultural daily *Tageszeitung,* and (more sensationally) Brandt's wife, Brigitte Seebacher-Brandt, writing in the conservative *Frankfurter Allgemeine Zeitung,* began the debate only weeks after the Berlin Wall fell.

Schneider faulted his fellow Leftists for having cast a blind eye to the inhumanity of the old East German regime. Seebacher-Brandt contended that while the Left might remain ideologically pure in opposing German unity, it could do so only at the cost of again being repudiated by public opinion. Novelist Günter Grass, rebutting Seebacher-Brandt and other Left revisionists, argued, on moral grounds, that Hitler had forfeited any German right to patriotism. Yet philosopher Peter Sloterdijk asked, with some surprise, "When were the Germans less ugly than today?" Writer Hans Magnus Enzensberger challenged the Left's (and his own previous) contempt for quotidian bourgeois concerns and contrasted the "hysteria" of elite Left intellectuals after the Berlin Wall fell to the "dimension of insight and common sense" displayed by middle-class East Germans "in an extremely tense and potentially dangerous situation." And various *Tageszeitung* writers began asking if the far Left really wanted to hang onto the axiom of the early 1980s' peace movement and support neutrality, when the far Right would like nothing better than a neutral status that would leave Germany's army unfettered by allies.

For the Left, the domestic reconciliation offered by German unification was a painful process; for the Center-Right it was a godsend. Kohl calculated correctly that West German taxpayers' grumblings were only temporary, especially since the flourishing West German economy could well afford investment in the GDR and would even benefit within a few short years from the "economic miracle" expected there. He gambled as well—by staking his personal prestige in vigorous engagement in the GDR election campaign—that all the polls predicting a Social Democratic landslide in the GDR were wrong. He reckoned that East German voters would be so fed up with any kind of socialism at this point that they would drop the region's prewar allegiance to the Social Democrats and elect conservatives. If so, then once the West German SPD's hopes of gaining a majority in the East were dashed, the Center-Left in the Federal Republic would be able to return the SPD to mainstream policy.

The SPD Left would not give up its foot-dragging on German unification until after East German voters did give conservatives the resounding victory that Kohl had hoped for. But by January 1990, the West German SPD would be forced by the East German SPD to endorse unification formally. This shift isolated the Greens in their lonely championing of two separate Germanys.

Events were pushing both Right and Left toward the center.

Chapter 4
2 + 4 = 1 Germany

On January 30, the Soviet Union and the GDR accepted the inevitable. Just before receiving Modrow in the Kremlin, Gorbachev declared to journalists that "no one ever cast doubt on the unification of the Germans." Two days later, Modrow presented his own plan for "reconstitution of the unity of Germany," but set German neutrality as a precondition. The West rejected this proviso, and the East German prime minister promptly downgraded his prerequisite to nothing more than a basis for negotiations.

Four days thereafter, at an enlarged Central Committee plenum, Soviet conservatives openly attacked Gorbachev for the first time over his policy on Germany.

This was the moment when any serious Soviet bid to veto NATO membership for a united Germany might well have succeeded. So long as there was no risk of war, foreign policy was no urgent concern of the man in the street. But East Germans took it for granted, random interviews suggested, that weapons are bad, neutrality is good, and the two Germanys would end membership in their respective military blocs as soon as they merged. West Germans, too, favored neutrality for a unified Germany, plus full American withdrawal from the Federal Republic, opinion polls showed.*

---

* Studies in March by the Mannheim Institute for Applied Social Research and the Institute for Social Research in Ann Arbor for the Friedrich Naumann Foundation recorded a high 50 percent in favor of neutrality and an even higher 57 percent for American withdrawal. See the German Information Center's *This Week in Germany,* April 13, 1990, p. 2.

Assessing the mood, then, analysts from across the political spectrum in West Germany believed that if a collision were to arise between NATO and German unity, as seemed programmed in February, NATO would lose. NATO enjoyed consistent 70 to 80 percent support in opinion surveys in the Federal Republic, but the assumption was growing that with the vanishing Soviet threat, NATO had finished its work and could now be dismissed. In West as in East Germany, conventional wisdom equated fewer weapons with more peace, and many voters (between 40 percent and 80 percent, depending on the phraseology in the questionnaires) were distressed by NATO's reliance on nuclear deterrence.

Moreover, a recurring strain of German self-pity—this time over the real lack of support for German unification by France and Britain at the end of 1989, and over the popularly perceived lack of support from the United States in American insistence on impossible German membership in NATO—had not yet dissolved into the energies required for the myriad practical tasks of union. If unity were really at stake, this environment too could have strengthened the urge to part with allies.

Here, the SPD was not the only question mark. Among West German conservatives, there were vestiges of old Gaullist longings (associated in the 1960s with Bavarian potentate and nuclear enthusiast Franz Josef Strauss). Some Western diplomats feared that even the Americanophile Kohl, whose most highly developed faculty was his instinct for the political jugular, might sacrifice NATO if anti-NATO sentiment developed in the Federal Republic.

As it turned out, latent Gaullism on the Right never found a spokesman. Misgivings about NATO on the Left did, in the persons of Egon Bahr on the SPD's own Left and the more weather-vane SPD Bundestag member Karsten Voigt. Moscow would never tolerate the slippage of the GDR into NATO membership, they contended (as did Mitterrand and a number of other, conservative European politicians, with somewhat different conclusions). Gorbachev was making so many concessions to the West that he was already under fire by hard-line domestic opponents for "losing" Eastern Europe, ran the analysis. If the GDR added insult to injury by going beyond neutrality to join the adversary alliance, that could be the end of Gorbachev and of detente in Europe. It was much too dangerous a gamble.

The SPD corollaries were implicit: If a united Germany could not be a member of NATO, that meant that *West* Germany would quit the Western alliance. And if the Federal Republic left NATO, Congress would surely pull back U.S. forces deployed in the Federal Republic and else-where on the continent. That several hundred thousand GIs remained in Europe forty-five years after the end of World War II was, in any case, something of a miracle; the slightest irritant would stimulate their return home. More than one Western diplomat was worried that the Soviets might finally achieve through weakness what they had never managed to accomplish through strength: severance from NATO of the alliance's most important (and hitherto most vulnerable) European member, with subsequent withdrawal of American troops and collapse of collective defense in Western Europe.

Yet continued U.S. presence in Europe was essential, the allied govern-ments agreed. Only the United States could provide insurance against Soviet nuclear missiles still targeted on Europe; and only the United States could carry out the third of NATO's missions as described by the alliance's earliest secretary-general, Lord Ismay, in keeping "the Rus-sians out, the Americans in, and the Germans down."

By 1990, it was no longer a question of keeping the democratically reformed Germans "down" as in the unreconstructed 1940s. But there was a more subtle need—which the West Germans consciously endorsed—for the American counterweight to growing German might to assure the anxious French, Italians, and Dutch that they would not be overwhelmed by the Germans. And for a West Germany whose legitimacy in foreign policy was still overshadowed by the memory of Hitler, there was an even more subtle need for a partner whom Bonn could work with to launch its own initiatives and minimize backlash.

For a quarter century, France had performed this function in Europe in a symbiosis in which the Germans provided economic clout, the French licitness. But with the new ascent of Germany in 1990, France was too small and parochial (and unwilling) to be Bonn's main friend in dealing with the Soviet superpower. Only the United States had the size and the range of global contacts with the Soviet Union to be able to affect Soviet thinking on German unification.

Washington tended to conceive of its own evolving role as mediating between Bonn and Moscow—and to view foreshadowed West German credits to the Soviet Union as a bribe to achieve unification. The trian-gular relationship was actually much more complex, however. To be sure, Bonn wanted Moscow's blessing, and surplus West Germany was far more able to help the Soviet Union financially than was deficit Ameri-ca. But the Federal Republic was also the Western country that first discerned in Gorbachev's stated goal of a "common European house" a real yearning to be part of Western Europe—and not just a trick to push the United States off the continent. And West Germany knew intuitively the psychological dangers should the Soviet Union be isolated from the West as Weimar Germany was ostracized in the Versailles peace treaty.

American spokesmen, including the president himself, averred that the West must not gloat over Soviet reversals. Germans went further, seeking to reassure Gorbachev that the Russians would be treated with dignity, as full Europeans.

The Genscher Plan

The first Western officials to define the parallel needs of avoiding humiliation of Moscow and confrontation between NATO and unification in West Germany were Foreign Minister Genscher and Kohl's security adviser, Horst Teltschik. As early as 1987, Genscher had counseled the West to take Gorbachev at his word—and had drawn the Reagan administration's suspicion for it. Now, a few short days after the melting of Soviet resistance to German unification, Genscher proposed an idea that Teltschik had floated in a previous press interview:

NATO would promise that after the German merger, it would not advance its troops or nuclear weapons onto the territory of the present-day GDR (in peacetime). During a transitional period of several years, the Federal Republic also would not move its forces assigned to NATO, as the bulk of them were, to that area. Further, the Soviet Union—which was already having difficulty absorbing soldiers returning from Hungary and Czechoslovakia and was housing tens of thousands of them in tent cities—would be able to keep troops in the GDR for another three or four years before removing them all.

The last point was as much arrogation as promise; even half a year earlier, no Western leader would have presumed to "offer" Moscow the opportunity to keep in East Germany for a few more years the forces it had stationed there for decades.

This package quickly became NATO's position. It extended NATO protection to the area of the GDR (though this was not immediately clear), yet still offered unilateral restraint. It could, the West hoped, save face for Gorbachev and let him argue to his domestic critics that NATO was not, as the Americans put it, "taking advantage of" the Soviet loss of empire.

At this point Bonn—already gratified by Bush's open support for German self-determination—urged the administration to shift from passive to active promotion of German unification. To this end, in early February, Genscher unexpectedly flew to Washington on the eve of U.S. Secretary of State Baker's scheduled trip to Moscow.

In one sense, the United States now had to make its most fundamental policy choice in deciding whether to commit its own prestige to promote operationally the cause of a German unification that France and Britain still dreaded. In another sense, the United States had already set its course two months earlier, when Baker had gone to Berlin to back German self-determination. Bush and Baker, both educated in New England, felt the New Englanders' affinity for the Old World, and their instincts in backing Europe and Germany the previous spring had been rewarded so far. After initially staking out ground to the right of Ronald Reagan in superpower policy, they had continued the evolution, begun in the last two years of the Reagan administration, away from interpreting every new concession from a weakened Soviet Union as nothing more than sly peace propaganda designed to lure Europe away from the United States. They did not feel the need to put the same impossible negative burden of proof on the West Germans that their predecessors (and the French) had repeatedly done in forcing the Germans to demonstrate that they were *not* neo-Nazis or were *not* striving for economic hegemony in Eastern Europe or drifting into an unholy new Rapallo conspiracy with the Soviet Union.

Moreover, the Americans were persuaded by Kohl's assurances and by the "Genscher plan," as it came to be called, that the West Germans had finally focused on the issue of NATO membership and were themselves determined to preserve this membership as a factor of stability in Europe. Baker's stipulation in Berlin six weeks earlier of German adherence to NATO was being fulfilled.

Then too, in the last analysis, the United States had no choice. The train of unification had left the station, as the Germans were fond of saying, and there was no point in lying down in front of the locomotive. The French and British did not yet acknowledge this reality. The Americans did.

Under the circumstances, Baker responded positively to the new German call to action—and then raised eyebrows by a rare slip in a postmidnight press briefing in Moscow in which he spoke of possible German "association" with NATO as an alternative to full membership. The State Department quickly smoothed over the gaffe, and Gorbachev politely paid little attention to it.

Hot on the heels of the secretary of state, Kohl and Genscher too visited Gorbachev. After their own talks with Soviet counterparts, they announced jubilantly that Gorbachev had "promised [them] unmistakably that the Soviet Union will respect the decision of Germans to live in one state, and that it is up to the Germans themselves to determine the time and the way of unification."

On the flight home, Kohl popped open the champagne bottles. Teltschik shortly declared that the key to German unity now lay in Bonn.

The Federal Republic's allies reserved judgment, and suspected that Kohl was interpreting the Kremlin's signals much too optimistically. NATO membership was only the most obvious controversy that remained unsettled.

At this stage, Soviet policy called for a united Germany to be neutral and demilitarized—and Gorbachev's earlier advocacy of continued occupation of Germany by Soviet and American forces was still on the table. Yet Moscow was not making a major pitch for this outcome. Gorbachev said nothing about neutrality in approving German unification on January 30, nor did he reinforce Modrow's concurrent bid for neutrality. He did not exploit Baker's subsequent faux pas, and he conspicuously did not go over the head of the Bonn government to court the West German Social Democrats as the Soviet Union had done in the early 1980s. Whether out of preoccupation with Kremlin infighting, the floundering Soviet economy, and Lithuania's gathering independence movement, or out of a hunch that German anchoring in NATO would actually best serve Soviet interests, Gorbachev initially let the issue ride. The most precise expression of the core Soviet concern, perhaps, was Gorbachev's assertion, a week and a half after his talks with Kohl and Genscher, that while the two Germanys had a right to unity, Moscow too had an "inalienable right" to ensure that reunification did not lead to "moral, political, or economic damage" for the Soviet Union.

By the time Gorbachev put some vehemence into his rejection of German membership in NATO in March and April (and even sought to reclaim a Soviet say in the internal aspects of German unification), it was too late.* Without having thought about it especially, West German

---

* See Fred Oldenburg, "Sowjetische Deutschland-Politik nach der Oktoberrevolution in der DDR," *Deutschland Archiv* 1, 1990, pp. 68–77, and Gerhard Wettig, "Stadien der sowjetischen Deutschland-Politik," *Deutschland Archiv* 7, 1990, pp. 1070–78.

citizens were convinced by then that the Soviet Union would not block unification over NATO. They simply ignored the Soviet nyet.

Even the SPD-West fit this pattern, if by a more conscious process. At this point, the party pragmatists vigorously contested the Left's thesis that the Western alliance must be disbanded and replaced by an undefined East-West "security order." The moderates won a partial victory; a week after the SPD-East lost the GDR election, the SPD-West would agree to NATO membership, if the alliance abandoned much of its existing strategy, and if membership were only provisional, pending establishment of that new pan-European security order.

2 + 4

The forum the principals devised to resolve differences over the "external aspects" of German union was a series of roving "two plus four" conferences of the foreign ministers of the two Germanys and the four occupying victors of 1945: the Soviet Union, the United States, Britain, and France. "Two" preceded "four" in the formula at American (and West German) insistence, to stress that the Germans were equal partners in the talks and were not being dictated to by the others.

In intense brainstorming before sounding out Moscow, the Americans and West Germans had considered prolonging four-power rights for as long as Soviet forces remained in the GDR, as a means of keeping an American sanction on Soviet deportment. But the West Germans, in particular, noted Soviet agreement to full military withdrawal from Hungary and Czechoslovakia. They trusted the inherent dynamics of Gorbachev's shedding of external burdens—as well as growing Soviet frustration with maintaining divisions in the GDR that were too few for military operations but exposed too many idle recruits to Western resentments and temptations—to ensure fulfillment of Soviet promises of pullback.

In the end, Bonn and Washington chose the cleanest option and specified that the special status of the four powers in Germany must not be protracted after unification. The only business of the six foreign ministers' consultations would be the restoration of full sovereignty to Germany and termination of the still nominally occupying powers' "rights and responsibilities" in Germany left over from the Potsdam Conference, the cold war, and the absence of any formal peace treaty ending World War II.

"Two plus four" could act as a clearinghouse on other issues, to shuttle them to appropriate venues, but would not itself negotiate them. It would report final results to the thirty-five-nation summit of the Conference on Security and Cooperation in Europe (CSCE) planned for late 1990, but the thirty-five would have no say in the conditions of German unification. Nor, at this late date, would there be any formal peace treaty that would put an onus on today's Germany and make it liable for reparations claims against Hitler's Germany from the dozens of real or formal belligerents in World War II.

With two plus four and the Genscher plan in place, the United States no longer needed to hammer home the importance of German membership in NATO; the Bonn government itself was now doing this. Washington could move on to champion the goal of German sovereignty (including the right to join alliances acknowledged by all signatories of the CSCE Helsinki Agreement of 1975).

The potential collision in February between NATO and German unity was thus deflected to a very different potential collision in March between full and limited German sovereignty. In this new context, Washington would not be tarred with blocking German unity. If Moscow turned adamant in refusing NATO membership, however, the Soviet Union would be tarred with blocking German sovereignty.

Prophylactically, the United States emphasized Bonn's old principle of the 1980s that there must be no "singularization" of the Germans. The Soviets had not yet focused on demanding that the pan-German army be limited to less than half the size of the two existing German armies. They soon would do so, however, and the United States wanted to head off any Soviet demand for a special ceiling on German forces outside the twenty-three-nation conventional arms-control negotiations in Vienna.

Additionally, both the Kohl government and Bonn's NATO partners wanted to avert any premature rush to huge unilateral German military cuts of the sort the Social Democrats were already proposing. These cuts would come as the nations distributed their collective "peace dividend," but the allies did not want to give away their bargaining chips before Gorbachev actually signed the first Vienna accord bringing the Warsaw Treaty's old superiority in tanks and artillery down to parity with NATO.

In a related issue, the United States moved beyond the very concept of parity to establish a new principle of inequality between the still-sturdy NATO and the disintegrating Warsaw Treaty Organization. For forty years, when the persistent Western aim had been to reduce Soviet su-

periority in heavy ground weapons, the goal of equivalence had provided a useful public shorthand in arms control. But now that Gorbachev
had agreed to parity (even if he had not yet signed on the dotted line
in Vienna)—and now that East Germans, Hungarians, Czechoslovaks,
and Poles were further reducing Warsaw Treaty strength by pulling their
armies out from the Soviet military command—the West wanted to signal that its voluntary political alliance should not be confused with the
old compulsory Soviet military alliance. NATO was not about to dis-
solve just because the Warsaw Treaty Organization was vanishing. It
intended to preserve a qualitative and not just a quantitative balance
between the Soviet power that would be withdrawing troops only 600
kilometers across relatively easy land lines of transport and the American power that would be withdrawing troops 6,000 kilometers across
the sea.

Washington therefore proposed for the next stage of arms cuts—and
Moscow accepted surprisingly swiftly—new reductions in military personnel that would leave equal American and Soviet numbers only on
the central front, while allowing the United States to keep an additional
30,000 troops elsewhere in Europe.

Deciphering Soviet Policy

An anomalous four months followed, in which official Soviet spokesmen categorically rejected German membership in NATO, while various Soviet semi-officials indicated privately to Western visitors that
Moscow would actually prefer not to leave an enlarged Germany as a
loose cannon, but would like to see it bound to NATO. Gorbachev would
not be able to voice this preference aloud, the moderate Soviets surmised, until after the battle for authority was fought out at the forthcoming party congress in July.

During this period, the West found it difficult to decipher which was
the real Soviet policy. This was an old conundrum, of course. Ever since
Leonid Brezhnev had decided that the oil crises of the 1970s were not
the death throes of capitalism and that a minimum of cooperation between the two systems was necessary for economic well-being as well
as for nuclear survival, contradictory motives had been at work in Soviet
policy toward Germany and Western Europe.

Defense, intimidation, security overinsurance, feelings of superiority
and of inferiority, justification of Soviet hegemony in Eastern Europe,
maximization of Soviet influence in Western Europe, gaining a Leninist

breathing space now the better to combat capitalism later, holding Western Europe hostage against U.S. strategic missiles, exorcising the trauma of World War II occupation, playing Europe against America, pushing America out of Europe, keeping the Americans in Europe to restrain the Germans, deciphering the sometimes enigmatic American super-power, persuading Europe to persuade America of particular poli-cies, tapping Western technological wizardry, then simply muddling through the multiple Soviet domestic crises—all these strands fed into declaratory Soviet policies that might develop in any of several directions.

By 1990, the puzzling out of Soviet policy was made even more difficult by the lag of official statements behind the logic of Gorbachev's "new thinking" and by the new cacophony of voices in Moscow. It was hard for Western military analysts to believe that the Soviet superpower, with its strategic nuclear arsenal and the largest army in Europe, really feared the fully civilianized and Europeanized Bundeswehr. If it did, however—and if Moscow wanted to avoid any urge by Germans to acquire their own nuclear weapons—then unofficial Soviet expressions of sympathy for German anchoring in NATO were prudent and made much more sense than the official Soviet policy of detaching Germany from NATO. And they were certainly matched by the explicit preference of the Poles, Hungarians, and Czechoslovaks for German membership in NATO, ex-pressed both unilaterally and in an unprecedentedly captious Warsaw Treaty foreign ministers meeting in mid-March.

In this context, official Soviet policy seemed inexplicably counter-productive. It could only increase the stakes in terms of Soviet prestige and make it ever harder for Gorbachev to reverse course eventually without losing face. Yet Gorbachev's and Shevardnadze's negative pronouncements and backtracking continued, and convinced numerous senior Western analysts that the Kremlin would not yield on NATO mem-bership, even if the Soviets shot themselves in the foot in their stand for Leninist principle.

Thus, in 1989, Gorbachev accepted the guideline of bringing Soviet and Warsaw Pact heavy ground weapons down to NATO levels—to the initial astonishment of the West—only to balk in 1990 at completing the Vienna negotiations to confirm this. Shevardnadze agreed early on in contacts with the United States and West Germany that there need be no formal peace treaty, but then resumed talking about a peace treaty at the first two-plus-four meeting. Shevardnadze paid an unprecedented, friendly visit to NATO headquarters one day, only to seek a loosening of Germany from it the next—by requesting German membership in both alliances, or perhaps political but not military membership in NATO on the French pattern, or perhaps Soviet membership in NATO.

The Soviet Union further slowed down its unilaterally planned withdrawals of troops from the GDR in 1990, and spokesmen vacillated between attributing the deceleration to technical problems or bargaining pressure on the West. Moscow proposed, variously, an "international" referendum on German unification; a leisurely decision on German unity a year hence by the thirty-five-nation CSCE; oversight by the Soviet Union (and other World War II victors) even over domestic aspects of German union; leaving external security arrangements ambiguous even after the two Germanys merged; no nuclear weapons in Europe; minimal nuclear weapons there; a kind of Guantánamo enclave of residual Soviet forces in eastern Germany; departure of all American troops from Western Europe as all Soviet troops left Eastern Europe; and continued stationing of Soviet and American troops on German soil. The Soviet suggestions seemed almost random; they never added up to any coherent alternative to the Western proposal.

Nor were unofficial Western conversations with Russians unanimous in their thrust. For every Vyacheslav Dashichev of Moscow's Institute of East European and Foreign Policy Studies—who told the newspaper *Die Welt* just after the GDR election that the NATO issue was not a major problem—there were dozens of contrary hard-line comments. And the latter issued from the more authoritative Soviet specialists on Germany, including current and former ambassadors to Bonn and the senior Foreign Ministry official on German policy.

Throughout this period, the West, with Bonn in the lead, opted to interpret each new Soviet rejection of German membership in NATO primarily as rhetoric for domestic Soviet politics—and to stick to the Genscher plan without budging. Genscher himself kept meeting with Shevardnadze both inside and outside two plus four; each time he declared afterward that the Soviet utterances were positive and Gorbachev had not yet said his "last word."

In part, the West German optimism rested on the assumption that Gorbachev would eventually choose the lesser evil of acceding to inexorable developments to gain international tranquility and German help with Soviet admission to the European club over the greater evil of bucking the trend and isolating the Soviet Union. And especially after the Baltic declarations of independence from the Soviet Union in mid-March, West German resolution in sticking with the Genscher plan rested on the judgment that Gorbachev's troubles were so severe anyway that whatever the West did could hardly increase them.

There was also considerable bluff involved in Bonn's wager that Gorbachev would, in the end, overcome the formidable political and psychological barriers to Soviet accommodation to history. Even if Gorbachev himself made the conceptual leap, no one in the West was sure that he could in fact hang on in the Soviet Union, and no one wanted to contemplate what the transition in Central Europe would look like without this unique Soviet leader.

CSCE

The one area in which the West gradually modified the Genscher plan to try to help Gorbachev save face was in "institutionalizing" CSCE. Beginning in February, Genscher energetically lobbied the United States to offer the Soviets a kind of pan-European security council that would guarantee them a voice in European affairs even after their troops left Eastern Europe.

Baker was skeptical. The CSCE had been a political football in the United States ever since its initial Helsinki conference got caught up in the ideological battles that eventually brought Ronald Reagan to the White House. The American Right considered the Helsinki Final Act of 1975 a sellout that legitimized Soviet-imposed postwar borders in Europe.

Yet in the intervening years, the minimal statement on human rights inserted into the Helsinki agreement at the insistence of the West Europeans stimulated astonishing ferment inside the closed East European regimes. A series of ad hoc review conferences kept the spotlight on repression of dissidents, and governments that acknowledged the legitimacy of foreign states' interest in their human rights performance kept releasing political prisoners in order to avoid international criticism. This, in turn, emboldened more citizens to discover and speak their minds.

The fateful Hungarian decisions to dismantle the barbed wire on the Austrian border in May and not to force East German emigrants to return to the GDR in August could both be traced to the moral suasion of CSCE. More broadly, Western assurances at Helsinki that the East-West borders were "inviolable" (though not "unchangeable," if peaceful means were used) had allowed Solidarity to spring up and demand domestic change in Poland without fearing exploitation of any resulting Polish crisis by German "revanchists." Helsinki—and the rise of the unorthodox Mikhail Gorbachev to lead the Soviet Union—paved the way for the peaceful revolution of 1989 throughout Eastern Europe.

In retrospect, the Americans acknowledged the political virtues of CSCE. In the realm of security, however, they certainly did not want utopias about vague collective security among erstwhile adversaries to replace NATO's proven collective defense among democratic friends. And, initially, they were wary lest Genscher slip into trying to substitute CSCE for NATO—or let Soviet troops stay on in the GDR without any departure deadline in an effort to help Gorbachev. Such an ambiguous arrangement, Washington thought, could threaten stability by generating pressures—from German citizens wishing to be rid of the Soviet forces—to get rid of Western allied troops as well, as a price for hastening Soviet withdrawal.

The United States therefore rejected any grandiose ideas of a European security council with real powers. Once the Americans were persuaded that Genscher intended CSCE to supplement rather than supplant NATO, however, and that Bonn would eventually pin down Moscow on the removal of Soviet divisions from the GDR, they saw no harm in elevating CSCE modestly. They agreed to the CSCE summit at the end of 1990 that Moscow had proposed—if the Vienna agreement on conventional arms control were already signed and ready to be blessed by the summit. They reckoned that giving the floating CSCE conferences some regularity—and even permanence in the form of a small secretariat—would do no harm. If this then helped Gorbachev sell Soviet retreat from East Germany and Eastern Europe in the Kremlin, so much the better.

The volatility of Gorbachev's and the Soviet Union's position might well have recommended caution (or paralysis) in the historic reunification of Germany. The West Germans decided, however, that loss of momentum constituted an even greater risk than leaping into the unknown. Events were more controllable if they were moving, they thought, than if an unpredictable GDR or Soviet Union were dead in the water. Besides, if Gorbachev might fall, that possibility should provide all the more reason to press ahead with unification before a hard line or sheer chaos returned in Moscow. Bonn, mindful too of growing unease among West German voters in the limbo before currency union about just how much they would be asked to pay, began accelerating things once again. This time, the Federal Republic floated the idea of full political union by the end of 1990.

The United States, despite some misgivings about West German disregard for bruised egos among the smaller European nations that had not been consulted in setting up two plus four, essentially backed Bonn in its choice of tactics and tempo.

Among the smaller nations, the most agitated was Poland.

Chapter 5
Denouement

The great postwar reconciliation still pending in early 1990 was that between Poland and Germany. Israel and West Germany had long since developed their "special relationship." France and West Germany had long since concluded their "alliance within the alliance," even if Mitterrand was currently possessed of the seven-year itch. Even the Soviet Union and West Germany had worked out a modus vivendi, and by the late 1980s Bonn was in many ways Moscow's most understanding partner in the West.

Only Poland, the country that had suffered the highest casualties per capita at the hands of the Nazis, remained unreconciled with today's Germans. The reason was the legally unsettled Polish-(East) German border, left over from the Potsdam Conference's awarding of the eastern third of prewar Poland to the Soviet Union, with compensating German lands attached to Poland in the west.

The Federal Republic had pledged not to change the boundary by force, both in its treaty of 1970 normalizing relations with Poland and, more generally, in the 1975 Conference on Security and Cooperation in Europe. Yet Bonn had always maintained that final recognition of the Oder-Neisse border would have to await a government that could speak for a united Germany. The West German conservatives, in particular, had stressed this legal position after they came to power in 1982, and some of the Bavarians in the CDU's sister party, the Christian Social Union, even insisted that the German boundaries of 1937—with Silesia and Pomerania still part of Germany—were the proper, legal ones.

Kohl consistently cited the legal reservation on the finality of the Oder-Neisse line, even when Foreign Minister Genscher and one bold Christian

Democratic MP had urged giving Poland firm political (as distinct from legal) guarantees on the permanence of the border.

In reality, the Polish border had been a nonissue for a long time. Despite occasional fiery rhetoric from the oldest generation, the once-powerful West German associations of the more than ten million postwar expellees from the eastern territories had, by the 1980s, been tamed into folklore and nostalgia clubs. The Federal Republic's overwhelmingly middle-class voters had no interest whatever in disturbing the peace to recover poor and polluted Silesian provinces. From November 9 on, Kohl's entourage was saying privately that it would soon become clear even to the expellee organizations that forfeiting impossible claims on Polish lands would be the necessary but small price to be paid for the incredible unification of the German heartland. The realization would just take a certain time (as well as Republican losses in regional elections) to sink in.

As one of his first acts after becoming the new non-Communist prime minister in Poland, Tadeusz Mazowiecki had joined with other Polish and German Roman Catholics in a placatory gesture in September 1989, signing an expression of sympathy for the suffering of expellees in the 1940s. Most Poles had no patience with the German waiting game, however, and in the early months of 1990, the Warsaw government kept demanding more and more explicit assurances—so insistently that it irritated even West German officials favorably disposed to Poland. The nadir of this interaction would be the brusque reception in May of that supreme conciliator, Richard von Weizsäcker, on the first visit ever made by a West German president to Poland.

The whole feud burst upon the American and international scene on February 25, in a joint press conference given outside Washington by President Bush and the visiting West German chancellor. After two days of shirtsleeve talks in Camp David, which the Germans valued as a sign of special bilateral closeness, Kohl repeated that only a freely elected parliament representing the whole of Germany would be the "legally competent sovereign" able to declare the finality of the border. "No one has any intention of linking the question of national unity to the change of existing border," he asserted. But despite a barrage of questions, and Bush's pointed intervention to state American recognition of the Oder-Neisse line, Kohl would not go further.

Back home in Bonn, the chancellor then compounded the offense by saying that Poles should not expect any reparations in the ultimate border settlement. In fact, Bonn had already given generous sums (some called it ransom) to Poland in the 1970s; reciprocally, Warsaw had let two hundred thousand ethnic Germans emigrate from Poland to the Federal Republic. But the raising of the monetary issue in the quarrel over the border did sound to outsiders like cheap haggling.

Something of an international fire storm broke over the question. Those who suspected the worst of the Germans saw their fears confirmed and vented all their anxieties in almost cathartic fashion. West German diplomats asked sotto voce whether the Germans had gotten so close to their goal of unity only to have Kohl rekindle all the old mistrust of Germans throwing their weight around.

In the end, the tempest served some useful functions. It won for the Poles a seat at the two-plus-four table for the discussion of their western border. It gave Britain and France a hook they could use to reengage in the diplomacy of German unification after their sulk of the previous four months. (Their lingering incredulity at their own drop in influence from the inflated political rank conferred on them by the cold war and Germany's prolonged semisovereign status prevented their taking full advantage of the opportunity, however. In the case of France, Mitterrand delayed his adjustment to reality with one last flourish in backing Polish demands that German unification be preceded by the peace treaty that was anathema to Bonn.)

Domestically, the flurry over Poland offered Kohl outside pressure he could apply to persuade his right wing to give up idle Silesian dreams for real Prussian unity. It elicited identical statements from both German parliaments renouncing claims on Polish territory, in pledges that awaited only the final seal by the future all-German government. It sparked public discussion about what needed to be changed in the West German constitution to forswear irredentist claims in the future. It chastened the West Germans into somewhat more subdued conduct in diplomacy. It induced the Bonn government to be more meticulous in soliciting European tolerance for each step toward unity, rather than confronting neighbors each time with a fait accompli. It convinced Kohl that—however unfair he might think it for foreigners to hold the Federal Republic to more exacting standards than other governments forty-five years after a war and holocaust that were not the doing of today's Germans—this judgment was a fact of diplomacy; to indulge in self-pity over the phenomenon would only aggravate resentments.

The Polish diversion may also have marked, finally, the return to normality for the Germans after World War II. It did not and could not remove the special demand for contrition by Germans for the sins of their grandfathers, nor the special responsibilities (as distinct from guilt) that German statesmen see history placing on them for decades to come. Yet, when it was all over, with the Oder-Neisse line guaranteed after all, with the united Germans still in NATO and still leading the drive for post-national European integration, a new era was opened. Prejudice against today's Germans based on brutal experience with yesterday's Germans, as one abruptly retired British cabinet member learned,* could no longer parade as prudence. Germany was no longer a political dwarf.

The Election Upset

External issues hardly impinged on the campaign for the March 18 election in the GDR. The feud about Poland's western boundary did not exercise East Germans, who tended to be more anti-Polish in personal contacts than the West Germans but certainly had no designs on the opposite banks of the Oder and Neisse rivers. Nor did the whirlwind of two-plus-four diplomacy find much resonance among voters focused on pocketbook issues.

Similarly, Kohl's curt treatment of Modrow during Modrow's visit to Bonn in mid-February and the chancellor's rejection of Modrow's and the roundtable's request for an immediate handout of 10 or 15 billion deutsche marks ($9 billion) seemed to agitate the West German media more than East German citizens. And the takeover by West German parties of the East German campaign seemed to attract rather than repel voters. They knew the Western politicians better (from television) than they knew their own, formerly reclusive, politicians, and they certainly trusted the West Germans more.

In this sense, Kohl's and Brandt's appearances in Erfurt and Rostock served to reassure the East Germans that Christian Democratic chairman Lothar de Maizière and Social Democratic chairman Ibrahim Böhme were not pawns of the Communists. Random interviews suggested that

---

* In an interview published in the *Spectator* of July 12, 1990, Secretary of State for Trade and Industry Nicholas Ridley called plans for European monetary union "a German racket designed to take over the whole of Europe." He compared the surrender of sovereignty it would entail with giving up sovereignty "to Adolf Hitler," and said the French were "behaving like poodles." By July 14, he was forced to resign.

voters complained about interference by West German politicians (if at all) only in the case of parties they opposed, but found it natural that Bonn politicians from whatever party they supported should help their colleagues in the east.

Actually, the massive West German intervention helped clarify the issues. The basic question was not whether the two Germanys should merge; that had been decided long since in the streets of Leipzig and Plauen. The major questions concerned only the when and how of unification—fast or slow, and with what kinds of social guarantees. In shorthand form, this was reduced to a debate over whether union should follow Article 23 or Article 146 of the West German Basic Law (constitution).

Although this distinction was somewhat artificial, it did pose to East Germans the choice of adhering to the West German constitution with few changes, or of starting with a tabula rasa, writing a new joint constitution, and reopening all the political as well as constitutional issues of the previous forty years. Conservatives, by and large, favored simple, swift accession under Article 23. Social Democrats, by and large, favored fundamental rethinking of Article 146 and the chance to reargue such hoary controversies as moving beyond democracy's traditional negative freedoms from coercion to positive socialist rights to work, housing, and the like.

The campaign ran largely as might have been expected. Kohl, fearing that the CDU-East might be blacklisted because of its decades as a satellite party of the Communists, insisted that the Christian Democrats form an alliance with two tiny new parties—a tactic that threatened to backfire just days before the election, when it was revealed that the chairman of one of these, Democratic Awakening, had been a high-ranking informer for the secret police. At rallies, the conservatives drove home their ability to deliver unification and money fast—and lost no opportunity to hang on the neck of the SPD-West the albatross of the party's earlier eagerness for dialogue with the old SED.

The SPD-West, after initial wariness about the total unknowns who had refounded the Social Democratic party in the GDR the previous fall, finally decided it had no choice but to back its namesake. It made the mistake, however (centrist Social Democrats complained), of identifying its main opponent as the conservatives rather than the old Communists. This turned out to be a total misreading of the mood of a population whose top priority was settling accounts with the old hierarchy.

The Communists, in their new clothes as the Party of Democratic Socialism, resigned themselves to a future minority position even before Modrow was voted out. They adopted the stance of a populist opposition, ready to lead strikes and highlight all the social and economic inequities of whatever transition the new government might attempt. And in the Volkskammer, they utilized the last days of their obsolescent majority to pass a series of laws—such as letting the old Communist bureaucrats review their personal dossiers to destroy incriminating material, and ensuring by trick clauses that profits from foreign industries owned secretly by the party would accrue to the party and not to common GDR coffers— that further revised the once-favorable Western view of Modrow. "A wonderful party!" mused SPD parliamentary leader Richard Schröder later about the Communists, as more and more such sleights of hand came to light. "Idealists at the top and all slit-ears [con men] down below!"

Historians might one day write a re-revisionist evaluation of the convinced Communist reformer who, at a critical point in the revolution, reassured both Gorbachev and the orthodox in Moscow that the Communists were not being ejected in the GDR. East German voters had no such perspective on Modrow.

With the fear of a Communist restoration almost gone—it would take the free election itself to vanquish fully the angst of decades—everyday worries dominated the campaign. It would be inaccurate to say there was a sobering of euphoria, since—apart from the very personal emotion of November 9 and a curmudgeonly grumbling about lack of support for unification from allies—there had been no national euphoria to begin with.

What did reign, though, was a sober, utilitarian yearning to join with Western prosperity and acquire the Western freedom to travel. East Germans fretted that they might get left behind in the unfamiliar Western free-for-all, but they calculated that the one thing worse than being exploited by West Germany would be not being exploited by West Germany. They therefore opted for what the orthodox Left derided as "deutsche mark nationalism" but the revisionist Left welcomed as a gain in common sense and a vast improvement over the old chauvinism.

On March 18, then, despite the earlier forecasts of a Social Democratic majority, the East Germans voted against social experiments of any kind and for the known economic and political success of the Federal Republic. The impressive 93 percent who cast their ballots gave a landslide 48 percent to the conservatives—more than double the Social Democrats'

22 percent. The Liberals, who immediately joined the conservative coalition, won 5 percent. The revamped Communists of the PDS got 16 percent. The various new-Left parties of the original revolution got a splintered 5 percent between them; other minor parties got 4 percent. The East German voters thus signaled their wish to unify Germany as fast as possible. Yet they also put a check on both East and West Germany's ruling conservatives in the form of a strong Social Democratic minority that the conservatives would need to engage in coalition before they could attain the two-thirds majority to amend the GDR constitution. It was a textbook finish, calculated to build stable democratic institutions.

A bitterly disillusioned Bärbel Bohley saw the conservative triumph as the end of the GDR's infant democracy, "with the voter behaving like a sheep again, yet fondly imagining he is taking part in his first free elections." East Berlin Communist reformers, still regarding political harmony as the desired norm and mistrusting a naked clash of "interests" as dirty, also echoed, unconsciously, Bertolt Brecht's sardonic comment, after the 1953 uprising, that the government needed to elect a new people.

Yet, for the majority, the process was profoundly moving. One woman said she felt almost "giddy" as she voted. A companion said he felt "awe" at doing something that really mattered, as he declared his political faith in democracy with his ballot. An octogenarian had a sense of seeing the world put right as she voted again in a free election for the first time since 1933. A nineteen-year-old political neophyte approved the "clarity" of the outcome.

Moreover, after forty years and the loss to the GDR of three and a half million people—a gaping fifth of the population—the ultimate vote of confidence was registered by foot. Emigration from the GDR after March 18 dropped to a third of its pre-election rate. The large majority of East Germans, it seemed, still saw a chance of establishing their identity—as fully franchised citizens of a united Germany.*

Aftermath

The grand coalition constituted itself within three weeks. De Maizière, who seemed to be the most stunned of anyone by his election as

---

* For a more comprehensively footnoted account of development in the GDR between fall 1989 and the March 18 election, see Elizabeth Pond, "A Wall Destroyed: The Dynamics of German Unification in the GDR," *International Security* 15, no. 2 (Fall 1990), pp. 35–66.

prime minister, turned out to be a "typical violist," amateur musicians noted, just irascible enough to stand up to the Christian Democratic paymasters in Bonn when he felt East German interests required it. He was an active Protestant layman of Huguenot descent, who became a lawyer after he was forced to quit his preferred career as a violist because of a nerve disorder. Since it was virtually impossible under Communist rule to be a practicing lawyer without party membership, he had joined the satellite party of the CDU, as the lesser evil, rather than joining the SED itself. In the process, he had evidently nurtured his independence.

De Maizière and his Social Democratic partners, pastor-turned-foreign-minister Markus Meckel and philosopher-turned-parliamentary-caucus-leader Richard Schröder, fit the axiom that East German conservatives are more Left, Social Democrats more Right, than their counterparts in West Germany. They formulated common positions on the approaching currency union, harmonization legislation—and even "provisional" NATO membership, if NATO changed—with a minimum of crises.

In its first sitting, the Volkskammer asked Israel for forgiveness for the Nazi holocaust against Jews and for the "hypocrisy and hostility" of earlier East German governments. In his first government statement, de Maizière approved full economic and social union with the Federal Republic by summer.

As the new dispensation settled in, there was no night of the long knives against the former rulers. There were, however, continuing revelations about the cruelties of the old regime and its Soviet patron. Only after the election did people who had been confined to psychiatric wards by the Stasi have the courage to recount their histories. Only after the election did those who had witnessed mass burials by the Soviet occupiers in the late 1940s dare speak out about them. Graves at Five Oaks, Fox Mountain, and other stations of the German gulag were dug up. Bones were unearthed, not only of old Nazis, but also of "class enemies" from the "bourgeois elite" who had fallen victim, an estimated eighty thousand in all, to famine and disease in internment camps in which prisoners' rations were deliberately reduced to below subsistence.

With the new East German government in place and moving rapidly toward German union, Mitterrand too accepted the inevitable. In April, he and Kohl kissed and made up, and launched a joint initiative to introduce European "political union" simultaneously with completion of the single market of 1992. Mitterrand further—after some blunt talk in Florida, in which Bush told him American troops would not stay in Europe as "mercenaries" if the European Community shut the United States out of political decisions—dropped his opposition to strengthening NATO's political role. NATO's declaratory shift to a less military emphasis was necessary to allay Soviet concerns, but it also implicitly perpetuated U.S. influence in Europe through NATO.

From May on, unification proceeded on the track laid down in the frenetic opening months of 1990. On May 5, the designated six foreign ministers held their first two-plus-four conference, in Bonn, and Shevardnadze floated the idea of leaving the external aspects in limbo for an unspecified time after Germany's domestic union. On May 15, the West German coalition broached substituting an all-German election for the West German election set for the end of 1990. Three days later, the two Germanys signed their treaty on currency union on the basis of a social market economy. The GDR guaranteed private ownership of property, free prices, and dismantling of state monopolies. The Federal Republic promised retirement, health, accident, and other social insurance.

At the beginning of June, at the superpower summit, Gorbachev lobbied once more for simultaneous German membership in both NATO and the Warsaw Treaty Organization. On June 1, the West German Bundeswehr and the East German National People's Army (NVA) agreed to establish official contacts between senior officers and units. West German Defense Minister Gerhard Stoltenberg specified that there would be one army only in the unified Germany, and that senior East German officers—who had been trained in the Soviet Union and practiced obedience to their Soviet masters second only to the Stasi devotion to the KGB—need not apply.

In an ironic twist, the loudest protests came from pastor and former peace activist Rainer Eppelmann, now the East German minister for disarmament and defense—a man who saw his new duty as preserving the jobs of all the generals and admirals under his wing. Professional West German soldiers, offended by Eppelmann's implicit assumption that all military hierarchies are interchangeable, no matter what system they serve under—and concerned lest Stoltenberg offer to take on junior NVA officers as a friendly gesture—let it be known that they would refuse to serve under undemocratic NVA officers.

For their part, West German generals made plans to turn the NVA into a local territorial army and worried not a whit that what had so recently been the best East European military machine in the Warsaw Treaty Organization might turn against NATO. Their main concern was to preserve the practice of conscription on the territory of the present-day GDR so that no zone might develop that could draw Germans out of the habit of the draft.

On June 12, the United States, Britain, and France agreed to give West Berliners a direct vote in the forthcoming West German (or possibly all-German) election. On the same day, Gorbachev proposed and Kohl rejected "temporary associated double membership" for Germany in both NATO and the Warsaw Treaty Organization.

On June 15, the two Germanys agreed that property nationalized after 1949, when the GDR government took over from the Soviet administration, would be returned to the original owners; the land reform of the early postwar years would be preserved, however, and adjustments would be made to avoid hardship for East German families living in buildings to be repossessed. On June 21, both German parliaments passed identical resolutions confirming the Polish border. The next day, two plus four convened its second session in East Berlin, listened to the military bands salute the dismantling of Checkpoint Charlie, agreed to conclude its work by the fall, and ignored Shevardnadze's surprise proposal that Western troops quit West Berlin within six months, while Soviet troops stay on in the GDR (and American troops in the Federal Republic) for five more years. The Soviet Union was "flexible," Shevardnadze said, responding amiably to his rebuff.

On June 26, the two German parliamentary presidents paid a joint visit to Israel to give assurances that the new united Germany need not be feared. The same day, *Pravda* published a remarkable manifesto by Shevardnadze that constituted the first public defense of his German policy against, as the foreign minister portrayed them, McCarthy-like zealots who might have avoided "losing" Eastern Europe by sending in the Soviet army. In the interview, Shevardnadze sought to put German membership in NATO in a more positive perspective after all the years of propaganda about German revanchism. "Here we need to clarify a few things," he said. "First, the FRG [Federal Republic of Germany] has long been a member of NATO. This means it can only be a question of increasing NATO's potential by the addition of the GDR when and if the latter becomes part of Germany. . . . We are by no means indifferent to Germany's future military-political status. But this question will probably be viewed differently depending on the changes which take place in Europe." These changes, he suggested, should include a less belligerent NATO, institutionalization of CSCE, and "substantial reduction in troops and armaments in Europe—including the reduction of the German military arsenal—to the level of defense sufficiency."

On June 27, Bonn guaranteed a $3 billion, twelve-year commercial credit to the beleaguered Soviet Union.

On July 1, in an organizational tour de force, the two Germanys began their currency and social union, without a hitch. East Germans picked up their deutsche marks at a favorable 1:1 exchange rate for their first 4,000 East marks—and prudently banked the money rather than going on a spending spree. West German goods flooded East German shops; price gouging appeared. East-West German border checks were dropped, while East German-Polish border checks were stiffened. Overnight, the lines of do-it-yourself Polish capitalists buying groceries for resale at cut-rate supermarkets in West Berlin vanished.

With currency union, Soviet troops in the GDR also began getting paid in deutsche marks, for the highest real wages they had ever earned, under Bonn's assumption of the GDR's financial obligations. In the broadest of hints, the Federal Republic offered to pay for building barracks in the Soviet Union so the Soviet army could be repatriated as soon as possible.

On July 2, the GDR coalition assented to all-German elections in December. On July 3, West Germany reduced military service from fifteen to twelve months. The same day, East German Foreign Minister Meckel proposed, to the void of the U.N. Conference on Disarmament, putting a ceiling of 300,000 on the combined German armed forces; removing all nuclear, chemical, and biological weapons from German soil; and letting Soviet forces stay on in the GDR for five more years. On July 6, a NATO summit in London, proclaiming that the Soviets were no longer "adversaries," invited Gorbachev to address the NATO Council; said its own task would henceforth be as much political as military; pulled back from its previous tenet of "forward defense"; and officially relegated nuclear missiles and bombs to "weapons of last resort."

Gorbachev and Shevardnadze responded positively from their ramparts at the all-important 28th Party Congress. Gorbachev did not manage to beat down his opponents at the congress, but then neither was he beaten down. He again received Kohl after the congress closed and on July 16—his alacrity once more caught the West unprepared—accepted German membership in NATO and departure of the 360,000 Soviet troops in the GDR within three or four years.

In return, Kohl promised, Br'er Rabbit-like, a ceiling of 370,000 for the joint German army—a number above what the Bonn government had expected to have to come down to anyway for domestic reasons. From Moscow's point of view, the figure represented a halving of the nominal 670,000 West and East German armed forces. From Bonn's point of view, the number sufficed to underwrite stability in the new era, and it was a significant improvement over the 250,000 the Soviets had first asked or the irrelevant 300,000 floated by Meckel. The Germans also extended their promise not to manufacture or possess nuclear, biological, or chemical weapons.

In the Soviet-West German deal, the Genscher plan was to prevail during the remaining stay of Soviet troops in Germany. No NATO structures or troops would be extended to the territory of the present-day GDR, but the American, British, and French brigades would remain in West Berlin. Once Soviet forces left, German forces under the NATO integrated command—but no nuclear weapons—could move onto the territory. And American forces could and should stay on in Germany, Kohl and Genscher noted. Within a few days, the Soviets acquiesced in this further inequality as well. Before the month was out, the first Soviet soldiers were applying to the Bonn government for asylum, and the first reports were coming in of stoning of Soviet troops by East Germans.

On July 17, two-plus-four, this time in Paris, agreed that Germany and Poland would sign a treaty guaranteeing the Oder-Neisse line. The Federation of Expellees called it a "total surrender of German areas and rights" in Poland and booed Kohl when he addressed the group.

In August, the United States announced that it would cut its armed forces by 442,000 over the next five years. Stoltenberg announced that the new German armed forces would draw 320,000 from the West German army, 50,000 from the East German army, and that the East German territorial forces would be commanded by West German officers.

On September 12, the last two-plus-four meeting, in Moscow, tied up the package. On October 3, the two Germanys would unify formally. On November 19, the CSCE summit would bless the most peaceful change of this magnitude in Europe's history.

Chapter 6
American Security Policy toward Germany

Germany—"the delayed nation," the rejecter of the Enlightenment, the political dwarf, the chronic worrier about its identity—is leading the way to the European future. The trek should normalize Germany, restore the European unity of Charlemagne, and, paradoxically, make this unity decentralized and federal as well as post-national.

The Bush administration has chosen well in rejecting the fears of national stereotypes to put America's full weight behind this metamorphosis.

The denationalized and decentralized Federal Republic (and therefore, vicariously, the GDR) is vastly better placed than France or Britain—not to speak of the Soviet Union—to enter the new Europe of the 1990s. The Germans already had to surrender their sovereignty and tribal patriotism in 1945, and so do not face that painful loss as the European Community assumes more authority. The Germans' social glue has long since passed beyond heroic nineteenth-century (and Nazi) chauvinism to the more humdrum but safer cohesion of consumer satiety and constitutional legitimacy. Today's policymakers in Bonn and Berlin come from the generation that was inoculated by the ache of discovering that their parents had tolerated Hitler's industrial murder of Jews and gypsies. And the Germans, with considerable powers already distributed to jealous Länder in a way that was not artificially imposed on them by the World War II victors but was an organic outgrowth of centuries of splintered principalities, will adapt nicely to the new regional dynamics as politics devolves downward as well as upward in the new Europe.

The lasting result of the concentric changes wrought by German unification should be a more relaxed political consensus in the Federal Republic itself, a new democratic as well as economic miracle in the GDR, and a qualitatively new experiment in cooperative endeavor in Europe. Western Europeans will strengthen the European Community to avoid being overpowered by the new Germany that will be a third more populous than France, Britain, or Italy. Northern Eastern Europe, attracted by the European Community magnet and the help in democratization it will get from Germany and perhaps Spain, will rejoin Europe. This continent will begin what promises to be a dynamic new European century.

In the end, both Germans and Europeans should emerge at peace with themselves in a way that they have not been since the Middle Ages (or perhaps ever). And the Russians should have access to this community so long as they do not try to claim membership by force of arms.

Germany is now a country whose time has come in a continent whose time has come again. It is the inheritor of the Enlightenment—and of the West—after all. It is the one country that has had a concept in these turbulent months of where it wants to go politically, and has executed a skillful foreign policy to get there. It has at last found its identity, in Europe as much as in unification. The result, far from excluding the United States from that cohering Europe, is giving America a more mature transatlantic contract.

"I think we *have* learned from history," mused one West German diplomat in the eye of the storm that swept away the cold war. He belonged to that generation of premature adults of 1945. He was speaking about Americans as well as Germans, and he was saying much more than this year's usual tribute to Americans of "We found out who our real friends are."

*   *   *

The Bush administration, priding itself on ignoring the foreign policy professionals and on flying by the seat of its pants, would be the last to admit that it had learned from history. But, by whatever process, it inherited some right choices from Ronald Reagan, and it made more right choices of its own on Germany and Europe.

Anyone rash enough to have made such an optimistic judgment before November 9, 1989, would have been dismissed as naive. Then, the consensus seemed to be that NATO was suffering from congenital and perhaps terminal crisis; that American and German interests were bound to clash as postwar Germany and its "successor generation" came of age; that only Moscow could offer reunification to the Germans, for a price; that (in the Right's formulation) Gorbachev was playing the peace and disarmament theme so cleverly that the West, swept up in "Gorbymania" and the fading Soviet threat, would outrace itself to disarm and leave Moscow to dominate Europe; that (in the Left's formulation) the United States could no longer impose bipolar confrontation on Europe; that the Americans would or should tire of paying for European defense and U.S. hegemony and go home; that the Europeans would or should respond by accommodating themselves to the Soviet Union. And if the further corollary that the old continent was suffering from "Eurosclerosis" no longer enjoyed currency, this was only because the Europeans had belatedly set 1992 as the target for a fully free internal market—though even here skeptics saw warning signs in the growing disenchantment with the European Community on the part of paymaster Germany.*

In part, the abrupt ending of German and European division in 1990 has transformed that earlier world; in part, it has exposed those premises as false, or at least incomplete.

Reagan and Bush

The first revision that hindsight compels in the old conventional wisdom concerns the role of the Reagan administration. The ideological slanging match over European exports of gas pipeline and pumps to the Soviet Union in the early Reagan years certainly was a nadir in U.S.-European relations. But the simultaneous U.S. insistence on deploying intermediate-range nuclear (INF) missiles in Europe as a response to new Soviet SS-20s and two decades of Soviet buildup of conventional heavy ground weapons in Europe was no American imposition on unwilling Germans. Nor did the controversial INF stationing and Reagan's Strategic Defense Initiative (SDI) destroy detente, as many Europeans and Americans had expected.

---

* For one of the most concentrated articulations of this view, see David M. Keithly, "The German Fatherland—of the Left," *Orbis* (Winter 1990), pp. 67-82. For the least apocalyptic of the pre-November 1989 studies, see Stanley R. Sloan, ed., *NATO in the 1990s* (Washington, D.C.: Pergamon-Brassey's, 1989).

On the contrary, the deployment was desired by two successive German governments to deflect Soviet nuclear intimidation, and it paved the way for Gorbachev's unprecedented "new thinking" and embrace of interdependence in foreign policy. The INF targeting of key Soviet command bunkers and other military sites, far from acting as a provocation to the Soviet Union (as the Germans had feared in a war scare that was far deeper and broader than Washington realized at the time), helped trigger the Soviet reassessment. In retrospect, it is clear that the Soviet failure to rally West German citizens against their government's INF deployments—and the threat of an exorbitant, open-ended race for Reagan's dream of SDI that the Soviets took far more seriously than did the American scientific community—helped Gorbachev convince the Politburo that it had to abandon the search for a security so absolute that it could only look threatening to neighbors. The result was the breaking of ancient Russian taboos in Soviet acceptance of on-site arms-control inspection and willingness to reach East-West parity by asymmetrical destruction of four times as many Soviet as NATO INF missiles and nine times as many tanks, artillery pieces, and armored vehicles.

Had a less ideological and more accommodating president been sitting in the White House at the time, the United States would undoubtedly have rewarded Gorbachev for these dramatic overtures—and would have risked freezing the Soviet evolution at an incremental, nonradical level. As it was, Reagan accepted the concessions as overdue, and asked for more. And at that stage of Soviet crisis, American obduracy, instead of triggering a palace coup against Gorbachev, pushed Gorbachev to wring more concessions out of his colleagues—and enabled Gorbachev's more radical advisers to wring more fundamental reform out of him. The process would end with that astounding ultimate concession of letting Eastern Europe and the GDR go their own way—and with Soviet reformers' condemnations of pre-Gorbachev Moscow that were scarcely less harsh than Reagan's own excoriation of the "evil empire."*

In his last two years in office, Reagan also furthered East-West rapprochement by his personal rapprochement with Gorbachev—and advanced European integration by the less orthodox means of a nuclear abolitionism that scared the Europeans into greater solidarity with each other. The occasion for the latter service was surely the oddest super-

---

* See Allen Lynch, "Does Gorbachev Matter Anymore?" *Foreign Affairs* 69, no. 3 (Summer 1990), pp. 19-29.

power summit ever held, at Reykjavik in 1986. In it, Gorbachev repeated the old Soviet proposal of ridding the world of nuclear weapons, and Reagan apparently agreed, quite casually.* Nuclear abolition certainly fit the logic of Reagan's SDI, which aimed to put antinuclear shields over the United States (and, by projection, the Soviet Union). It took the explicit talk of abolition of nuclear weapons at Reykjavik, however, for the implications to sink in fully with European leaders. Both the British and French nuclear missiles would be neutralized under any successful regime of superpower strategic defense, and so would America's extended nuclear guarantee for Germany, which rested on the ability of American retaliation to penetrate Soviet defenses.

Reagan's cabinet immediately retracted its commander in chief's utopia, in any case, but the president's willingness to give up the nuclear umbrella for Europe, without any prior consultation with the Europeans, helped stimulate one of the revivals of the dormant West European Union and added at least marginally to the push for a single European Community market in 1992 to help insulate Europe against American vagaries.

The Bush administration rejected Reagan's strategic assumptions about Europe but built on his tactical heritage. It exhibited none of the neo-isolationist yearning of Reagan's Sun Belt team to shed commitments to an ungrateful Europe and gain the freedom to intervene unilaterally elsewhere in the world. It took for granted the primacy of Europe in American foreign policy. It may not yet have shared the West Germans' strategic perception that the Russians were finally reexperiencing Peter the Great's longing to join Europe. But then neither did it display the Reagan and Carter administrations' corrosive suspicions of Germany's loyalty to the West that risked becoming self-fulfilling in stimulating German resentment of constant mistrust.

Bush's own first policy decisions on Europe were tactical, made in response to Polish and Hungarian reforms, the ongoing feud with Bonn over upgrading the Lance short-range missile, Gorbachev's coups in public relations, and the bad press Bush initially drew in the United States as a do-nothing president. At the NATO summit of May 1989, Bush ostentatiously seized leadership of the West by proposing more radical cuts in conventional arms in Europe, by promoting the Federal Republic to America's leading European partner, and by approving European inte-

---

* See Strobe Talbott, *The Master of the Game* (New York: Alfred A. Knopf, 1988), p. 325.

gration fully, without the reservations of his predecessors. In addition, he endorsed the shift of emphasis in NATO already worked out by alliance bureaucrats in downgrading military deterrence and upgrading political crisis prevention and management.

By the time November 9, 1989, shattered the forty-year-old postwar regime, then, the policy questions in Washington included not only the familiar "Can we trust the Germans?" but also "Do we continue the policy we have already laid down?" Although the answer was seen by many in American political circles as letting the German tail wag the American dog, Bush opted for consistency, self-determination, and a second chance for Germany over genetic determinism. The United States supported unification, prescribed NATO membership for a united Germany, and assured the Europeans that it would stay engaged in Europe for as long as the Europeans wished.

Bush's policy choices in February 1990 were more complex. They entailed not only endorsement of Bonn's acceleration of unification, but also initial decisions about the whole shape of the future security "architecture" in a very new Europe.

At that point, many senior voices were counseling many different courses of action or inaction. The father of containment, George Kennan, was urging the United States to proceed with the utmost caution and postpone all decisions for several years. Historian John Lewis Gaddis, convinced, like so many others, that the Soviet Union would never accept German membership in NATO, was arguing that the best solution would be double German membership in both NATO and the Warsaw Treaty Organization.

Stanley Hoffmann, chairman of Harvard's Center for European Studies, foresaw the end both of an American-dominated NATO and of German acceptance of U.S. occupation of Germany. He advocated emasculating NATO to its 1949 origins, before an integrated military command was set up. In his scenario, the United States would maintain its nuclear guarantee and conventional presence in Europe, but the main institutional link to Europe for the superpowers would be a strengthened CSCE that would keep both of them at arm's length. Primary responsibility for West European security would be assumed by a new West European defense organization, and the British and French would supplement American deterrence by extending their own nuclear umbrella over Germany.

A distinguished Harvard colleague of Hoffmann's proposed that Germany belong to NATO but be largely disarmed. Former national security adviser and present Georgetown professor Zbigniew Brzezinski envisaged a period of perhaps twenty years in which NATO and Warsaw Treaty forces would stay on in their respective Germanys. University of Chicago strategist John Mearsheimer, worried that the stable bipolar world was going to revert to an unstable scramble for balance-of-power advantage, went so far as to urge Germany to acquire its own nuclear weapons. Columbia University political scientist Jack Snyder, concurring in the widespread view that NATO was bound to vanish as the Soviet threat and Warsaw Treaty Organization vanished, proposed primary supervision of German confederation by the European Community, warned against any union of the two German armies, and sought perpetuation of two German states with guarantees of their sovereignty by the superpowers. Various others, presuming that the Germans would ask American forces to leave once the country was unified—but also presuming that stability required continued presence of U.S. forces in Europe—contended that France would have to give up its quarter-century distance from the NATO military command and invite American divisions to France.

Recommendations from Europeans were equally diverse, ranging from Otto von Habsburg's proposal for a full European Federation* and German Social Democratic plans to substitute a CSCE system of collective security for NATO's collective defense to Mitterrand's ambivalent wish to ensure the continued presence of Americans in Europe while reducing America's (and Germany's) political influence through a new East-West European "confederation" with Gaullist overtones.

In the end, Bush rejected all radical innovation in the institution of NATO, on the grounds of the old American adage, "If it ain't broke, don't fix it." He raised smirks for stating that now that the Soviet Union was not the threat it used to be, NATO's main enemy was instability. But this longest-lasting alliance in history did give the United States a familiar channel for insuring Western Europe against sudden dangers from any Soviet relapse to military intimidation, acquisition of nuclear weapons by militant Soviet minorities, ethnic shoot-ups between East Europeans no longer restrained by Pax Sovietica, or even an overbear-

---

* Interview with Otto von Habsburg, head of the House of Habsburg and member of the European Parliament, in "A Tale of Two Empires," in *The World Today*, May 1990, pp. 94-back inside cover.

ing Germany. Moreover, NATO existed and had become a habit in American foreign policy. It did not have to be invented, and American public support for it did not have to be created from scratch. U.S. troops would clearly be reduced in Europe under the new conditions, but voters' willingness to pay for them would not have to be generated anew.

The Bush judgments were ratified in July 1990 by the NATO summit, which declared that instability, not the Soviet Union, was the enemy, that nuclear weapons were only a last resort, and that (by implication) all remaining ground-based nuclear weapons would be negotiated away in Europe. Skeptics continued to foresee the demise of NATO, and to expect that Germany, once united, would show the door to Western allied troops.*

---

* See, e.g., Ian Davidson, "Atlantic alliance fails to read the writing on the wall," *Financial Times,* July 12, 1990, p. 2.

Chapter 7
Agenda for the 1990s

Given the fundamental U.S. policy decisions on German and European security that were made last December, February, and June, the remaining choices facing the United States smack of anticlimax. Yet the sensitive implementation of those earlier decisions is crucial, in nurturing the new NATO, fostering the most helpful environment for adjustments to German unification, supporting integration of the European Community, building CSCE structures, and providing economic underpinnings for the emerging democracies in Eastern Europe. In brief, a coherent U.S. policy should look approximately as follows:

NATO
Reports of NATO's death have been grossly exaggerated. The alliance seems fated to endure through the 1990s and possibly well into the twenty-first century. It is too useful to too many nations to be given up lightly, now that the Russians have not vetoed it. And the remarkable speed of NATO's adjustment to post-cold-war conditions—only one consensual year, as contrasted with the contentious four-year process of moving from massive retaliation to flexible response in the 1960s—attests to a strong will to keep NATO alive. Already NATO in its London summit in July 1990 has moved from a defense orientation to what it calls a more "political" focus on crisis management.

As long as the Germans and other Europeans still wish to perpetuate the alliance, then, the United States should continue to treat NATO as the primary forum for discussing security issues among the industrialized democracies. It should also seek to broaden NATO's reach, following the recent accreditation of a Soviet ambassador to NATO, by proposing that the alliance invite Japan to establish a permanent liaison office in Brussels. And it should promote various other innovations ranging from introduction of multinational forces to adoption of German as one of the official NATO languages to possible nomination of a European as NATO's supreme allied commander.

*   *   *

The many recent predictions of NATO's demise derived essentially from two related changes: evaporation of the Soviet military threat to Western Europe and German recovery of full sovereignty in the process of unification. The first, it was said, would remove Europe's need for American defense or deterrence and reduce U.S. influence in Europe. The second, combined with the first, would enable the Germans to end the occupation of their country by foreign (especially American) troops.

As 1990 presented NATO with a clean slate in security arrangements, though, Europeans reacted differently than anticipated. The most important player, the Center-Right government in Bonn—which seems certain to be reelected in December 1990—does not see a continuing although reduced American military presence in Germany as onerous. On the contrary, it says clearly that it wants to prolong NATO and the security insurance provided by American and other allied troops in what is now the Federal Republic.

But are the Germans just biding their time to ease the path to unity? Once they have merged, as various non-German analysts expect, will they then consider NATO a shackle that is doing little but keeping the "Germans down"? Will they expel American forces or dilute their own commitments to NATO so much that the alliance will turn into little more than a zombie?

Such an about-face seems unlikely for the present Bonn government. To be sure, its current enthusiasm for NATO could be unduly colored by gratitude for America's stalwart support for unification and the leverage this gives Germans against the more fickle French and the European holdouts of the British. But there will probably continue to be issues on which German and American perceptions are closer to each other than to those of France or Britain, and Germany will value its augmented influence in European councils arising from its American connection in NATO. In addition, Germany will appreciate America's bilateral and multilateral backing in dealing with the Soviet superpower. A nation that exports a third of its GDP does not casually surrender allies and allied amplification of its own policies.

Further, while American support of the sort accorded Bonn in the months since November 18 would be welcome to any European government, it is especially welcome to a German government that has yet to restore its full foreign-policy legitimacy after Hitler. In the same way that the French-German relationship and European Community "political cooperation" gave Bonn the cover to resume a discreet role in foreign affairs in the 1960s, 1970s, and 1980s, so the American-German relationship will allow Germany to promote policies unobtrusively in the 1990s that might otherwise attract domestic or foreign criticism. And such help from a NATO insider at early stages of policy formulation would be much more effective than help from an outsider operating only bilaterally or on the fringes of the European Community.

Nor are the German Social Democrats likely to behave much differently when they return to power in the 1990s or early 2000s. A governing SPD is always more conservative than an opposition SPD in any case, and it would tend not to tamper with the system it inherited unless a major crisis compelled doing so.

Besides, public opinion is hardly clamoring for radical change. Security concerns come low on the Germans' list of worries.* The first American troops to be withdrawn as forces are cut in Germany are being taken out of the large cities, where a military presence causes the most frictions, while in the smaller towns Germans are eager to keep American troops as long as possible because of the civilian jobs they generate. And the everyday irritations of the din of low-flying training exercises and the traffic delays as convoys clog the autobahns are diminishing in any case as the threat of war recedes and preparations for Armageddon diminish proportionally.

The upshot is that for Germans who had to surrender all their sovereignty in 1945, regained only incomplete sovereignty in 1954, and willingly gave up much of that to coordinate economic policies in the European Community, sovereignty is not seen as an absolute that allied

---

* Typically, no security issue even makes it into the top dozen problems bothering voters. In the May poll by Emnid for *Der Spiegel* and ZDF-TV, worries ranged from environmental protection (77 percent) to stimulating the East German economy (26 percent), but included no concern about war and peace. *Der Spiegel,* May 28, 1990, p. 22.

foreign forces violate by their presence. German and, for example, French instincts in this regard are quite different.

France, in fact, is the one large West European nation that has an urge, however ambivalent, to see NATO dwindle into nonexistence. German unification is shattering Paris's decades-old hope that when the cold war finally ended and the Americans left Europe, France would be the continent's natural leader. With its head, France therefore wants to preserve the American presence in Europe and NATO as a counterweight to block Germany from becoming the European superpower. Yet with its heart, France still sees the United States rather than Germany as its main rival. It therefore resists enhancing the role of Washington or of NATO's U.S.-dominated integrated military command that France quit in 1966. Nor does it want NATO to gain in political influence at the expense of the European Community.

The attitude of other major NATO members corresponds more closely to German than to French views. Most of the West Europeans are relieved by the perpetuation of NATO and the American voice in it, precisely because this affords them the maximum leeway to resist German domination. All the Europeans complain at different times about the propensity of the United States to practice divide-and-rule tactics in dealing bilaterally with NATO members before resolving issues in joint NATO sessions—and they protest when they see the United States act unilaterally, without advance consultations, and then try to browbeat allies into agreement. Viscerally, though, other allies currently worry less about the Americans than about the Germans. The United States is seen at present less as a bully than as an equalizer.

Moreover, when emergencies arise, European governments are frequently reluctant to cede leadership to other Europeans, or to exercise the kind of leadership themselves that might risk their domestic consensus. In such cases, the United States is still the ideal point man—to be followed if all goes well, and corrected if it does not. As the NATO maxim has it, the Europeans love to be led by the United States, just so long as it is in the direction the Europeans want to go.

The first test not only of the new superpower relations in the 1990s, but also of the new West-West relations in NATO, came with Iraq's lightning conquest of Kuwait in August 1990. The first consequence of this vivid reminder of post-cold-war threats to European security was to slow down NATO members' race to "renationalize" security decisions and disarm unilaterally. The second consequence was to forge a remarkable

Western, Soviet, and United Nations consensus that strong measures were justified to punish such aggression. Initially, at least, this case contained few of the ambiguities of Reagan's controversial bombing of Libya that so roiled U.S.-European relations in the mid-1980s. And the European allies displayed none of their earlier strenuous resistance to U.S. efforts to coordinate Western "out-of-NATO-area" moves. They willingly used NATO as well as Western European Union and European Community channels to impose an embargo on Iraq and join with the Australians in assembling a combined naval force in the Gulf. And the Federal Republic, the most resistant to economic sanctions and to previous unilateral U.S. military operations under the Reagan and Carter administrations, this time did not criticize American and British challenges to vessels suspected of breaking the embargo on Iraq.

To be sure, Bonn did not contribute as much to the common cause as the United States would have wanted; even centrist Germans who wished to accommodate the United States and also wished to see greater eventual use of German servicemen in peacekeeping outside of Europe maintained that the new Germany needed time to move in this direction. Yet under the roof of NATO agreement to put pressure on Iraq, West Germany did send minesweepers and supply ships to the Mediterranean to free other vessels for the allied expeditionary force in the Gulf, contributed $2 billion to the American operation and to those nations hardest hit by the embargo of Iraq, permitted use of bases in Germany for ferrying troops and materiel to the Gulf, and loaned some unique tanks for detecting chemical weapons to the United States for use in Saudi Arabia. This action, which would formerly have fueled editorial polemics for weeks about its constitutionality, roused so little controversy this time that it was all but wiped off the front pages by the concurrent squabble over the date for all-German elections. And Kohl pledged that he would tackle the constitutional issue immediately after the December election by proposing an amendment that would explicitly endorse sending German forces to other continents for collective peacekeeping purposes.

It could be, of course, that the present German honeymoon with NATO is temporary. Michael Stürmer, director of the West German Science and Policy Foundation, one of the Federal Republic's most prestigious think tanks, pleads passionately for continued American presence in Europe at this point for the very specific task of turning "the German question from a divisive burden to the engine of Europe." It could be that this mission will be accomplished within a decade, and that the united Germany will be so well assimilated into the new Europe by the turn of the century that American engagement in NATO will no longer be needed. But the time for both Germans and Americans to make that judgment lies in the future. Certainly, for the 1990s, active U.S. participation in NATO is seen by both partners as necessary to smooth the transition to a unified Germany—and as serving America's interest in maintaining a tranquil Europe.

*   *   *

On more specific policies, the offer to Japan of observer status in NATO could begin to fill the gap between Japan's major economic and financial role in the world and its minor security role. Japan's earlier acceptance of discussions of security issues in the Group of Seven annual economic summits suggests that Tokyo might also welcome more regular contact with NATO on these matters. Such contact could begin to fill in the Japanese-European leg in the triangle of industrialized democracies—a connection that has been far weaker than the U.S.-European or U.S.-Japanese link.

The desirability of having multinational forces in NATO—probably at corps level on the central front, with constituent divisions retaining national coherence—has already become part of conventional NATO wisdom in the course of 1990. This would presumably accelerate NATO's sluggish drive for standardization and "interoperability" of equipment. It would presumably redistribute the burden-sharing, so that Americans would not feel that they were paying so much more than Europeans for European defense. It would allow various European nations, if they wished, to maximize their shrinking defense budgets by specializing their forces without having to spread their resources thin over full armies, navies, and air forces.

Most important, multinational forces would relieve Germany of the stigma, as overall forces are reduced but NATO still needs to maintain rapid-action units on the central front, of being the only NATO member with foreign troops on its soil. German troops could be stationed elsewhere in multinational brigades or smaller units, even as allied forces were stationed in Germany.

Even though NATO members agree that this would be a good step, no action has yet been taken. This is, therefore, an area ripe for American leadership.

Adoption of German as an official language of NATO along with English and French would be a small gesture with large implications. One of the few remaining symbols of Germany's old second-class status in the Western alliance has been the requirement that German diplomats speak English or French when making official presentations in the NATO Council. And while German officials accredited to NATO are always fluent in English and/or French (and, in the case of the present ambassador, Finnish), the slight rankles. It would, of course, increase alliance paperwork and bureaucracy to some extent. But this disadvantage would be far outweighed by the full recognition it would accord the alliance's most important European member.

An American suggestion that a European assume command of NATO forces might disclose that the European members of the alliance could not agree on a European commander. A German, though the most logical candidate, would probably still be unacceptable to non-Germans; France is not in the integrated command; Britain is still too resistant to European integration to fill this post with appropriate political conviction; and an Italian would probably be regarded by others as too steeped in the thinking of the southern flank to be entrusted with the central command. Further, even though this consideration is becoming less important with improving East-West relations, only an American commander would have ultimate access to U.S. nuclear weapons should that last resort become necessary. An American commander may therefore continue to be the best solution for some years to come. As military drawdowns proceed, a European commander will come at some point, however, and it would be good to start thinking about this shift now.

There remains the question of whether the German army should continue under NATO command. Certainly there is no groundswell to reclaim German sovereignty by reclaiming national command of the Bundeswehr equal to national commands of the American, British, Italian, and other NATO contingents; in fact, the large majority of Germans is probably unaware of the unique arrangement for German forces. And German officers might actually prefer this arrangement as a way to avoid wrestling out domestic political consensus in a population that still tends to associate armies with Hitler's aggression and regard them as evil. Yet, after the bumpy democratization of security policy in the early 1980s in the form of the antinuclear movements, there probably can be no simple reversion to acceptance by the silent majority of whatever security policy the government chooses.

Logically, the United States should probably want the German government to take full political responsibility for the Bundeswehr at this point, just to avoid situations in the future in which the United States might be blamed disproportionately by the German public for unpopular military decisions that the German government actually concurs in. Politically, though, German assumption of full command of the Bundeswehr would make Germany's neighbors very nervous. And it could give the wrong signal, suggesting a trend away from the present, healthy Europeanization of foreign and security policy back toward nationalism.

Probably the best U.S. policy, therefore, would be to follow German instincts on the issue.

As a final point on the political-military level of policy, the perennial observation still holds that American consultations with allies should precede actions that affect the allies.

CSCE

Forebodings about a supplanting of NATO by a vague pan-European CSCE security regime are as exaggerated as reports of NATO's death. Fears of resort to an ineffective system of collective security in which all would formally be allied with all—and therefore none would come to the defense of any—address a straw man. The only period in which some Germans might have inclined to such a regime would have been in February 1990, before Kohl articulated his alliance policy and before the Russians accepted membership of a united Germany in NATO.

For the foreseeable future, German officials want to institutionalize CSCE, but not in a way that would conflict with NATO. In this framework, a strengthened CSCE is very much in the American interest in promoting standards of democracy and potentially providing some kind of a peacekeeping mechanism to fill the security void in Eastern Europe left by the retreat of Soviet forces.

Conventional Forces

The threat from Soviet superiority in heavy conventional weapons on the East-West fault line, the area with the heaviest concentration of opposing military forces in the world, perpetuated the cold war. When Gorbachev moved to cut Soviet armor unilaterally in December 1988, and multilaterally in the Vienna talks in 1989, the cold war therefore entered a truce. It ended altogether with the political transformation wrought by German unification. Yet everyone's policy for conventional arms and arms control still lags far behind this tectonic political shift.

For the West, the trick now will be to strike the balance between maintaining prudent military insurance against unpredictable threats to peace and distributing the anticipated "peace dividend" fairly as allies race to reduce their armies and defense budgets. The main Western forum for managing this joint task is still NATO. The main East-West forum for doing so is the Vienna arms-control negotiation on conventional forces in Europe (CFE) between the twenty-three members of NATO and the Warsaw Treaty Organization.

For NATO, the coming reduction in forces—the ultimate extent of agreed cuts is not yet known, but 50 percent of current levels is widely discussed—will require, above all, changes in the tactics of "forward defense" as they have been practiced for decades. These highly unusual military tactics of, in effect, defending every inch of West Germany's front line (rather than falling back under any attack to trade space for time) were decreed by geography. The key territory to be defended, that of the Federal Republic, was very shallow east to west, and cession of a few tens of kilometers in the east would have surrendered a third of the West German population. Moreover, once France left NATO's integrated military command, there was no further space for NATO troops to fall back to. Forward defense in the face of Soviet conventional ground superiority put uncomfortable requirements on NATO, compelling fast deployment of forces into forward positions in periods of danger so they could dig in sufficiently to withstand the assault of blitzkrieg-oriented Soviet forces.

Under the circumstances, NATO's greatest military fear for decades was that of a "standing start" attack by the twenty Soviet heavy divisions based far forward in the GDR. In fact, it gradually became clear after resolution of the 1958-61 Berlin crisis (and building of the Berlin Wall) that the Soviet Union had no intention of attacking Western Europe. Even purely militarily, its traditionally conservative assessments meant that the Soviet Union would never launch a premeditated attack without strong assurance of a swift victory that would avoid stalemate—and not give its East European clients time to defect and begin sabotaging Soviet lines of communication. And NATO forces, despite their conventional inferiority, always had enough defensive power to block such swift Soviet conquest.

Nonetheless, the Soviet buildup on the central front of ever greater leads in tanks, artillery, and armored personnel carriers—up to two and a half times NATO holdings in some categories—alarmed NATO because of concurrent Soviet efforts to coerce Western Europe into accommodating the Soviet Union politically under this military intimidation. The Soviet attempt to veto the NATO INF deployment in the early 1980s was the last intense effort of this sort.

Gorbachev's new willingness in 1989-90 to come down to parity with NATO in tanks, artillery, and armored personnel carriers at slightly below existing NATO holdings was, therefore, a major overture to East-West conciliation. It envisaged destruction of nearly two-thirds of all Soviet heavy weapons west of the Urals.*

Codified in preliminary agreement in Vienna, this "CFE I," as it has been nicknamed, has yet to be signed, as of this writing. When the opening of the Berlin Wall set off East European defections from the Warsaw Treaty Organization the tentative deal was overtaken by events. Poland, Czechoslovakia, and Hungary, despite their continued formal membership in the Warsaw Treaty Organization, have, to all intents and purposes, become neutral. The "sufficiency rule" proposed by the West before the East European revolutions—limiting any single alliance member to no more than 60 percent of its alliance's total holdings of artillery or other weapons categories—thus skews against the Soviets the original NATO-Warsaw Treaty Organization balance.

Under that rule, for example, only 12,000 of the 20,000 tanks allotted the Warsaw Treaty Organization could be Soviet. Yet Soviet generals can no longer count on the remaining 8,000 Polish and other tanks as part of their Warsaw Treaty Organization forces. Moscow has not rescinded its earlier agreement in principle to the sufficiency rule, but it is now balking at implementing it and is asking for the right to retain 70 percent or 80 percent of total Warsaw Treaty Organization weapons. Some Western flexibility would seem justified here, even if the East European nations would like to keep the 60 percent figure to apply maximum pressure for Soviet withdrawals from their territory.

Even in anticipation of a CFE I treaty, NATO began altering its forward defense in significant ways. Defense of eastern Germany will be left to lightly armed (East) German territorial forces under West Ger-

---

* See Jonathan Dean, "The CFE Negotiations, Present and Future," *Survival* 32, no. 4 (July/August 1990), pp. 313-24. Dean, arms-control adviser of the Union of Concerned Scientists and a former head of the U.S. delegation to the Mutual and Balanced Force Reduction Tal' s, has consistently been the most thoughtful conceptualizer of how conventional arms control might proceed. See also Dean's *Meeting Gorbachev's Challenge: How to Build Down the NATO-Warsaw Pact Confrontation* (New York: St. Martin's Press, 1990).

man command; NATO troops will not enter this region during the remaining three or four years of continued Soviet presence, and even thereafter NATO forces (along with tactical nuclear weapons) will probably still not be stationed there. Germany's new eastern border will not be fortified against neutral Poland and Czechoslovakia, even to the discreet levels of NATO's previous preparations along the East-West German border. NATO's regular large military exercises, which were previously necessary to maintain readiness for sudden forward defense, have already been cut in half, and will be cut further. And the barrage of noisy low-level jet passes by NATO pilots to practice underflying radar in Central Europe's clouds has diminished and will diminish further. These trends will continue as Soviet withdrawals progress and as allied troops are drastically thinned out in Germany.

All this should help reduce everyday military-civilian and American-German irritations arising from the stationing, over two generations, of a million German and foreign soldiers in cities and villages in a thickly populated area no larger than the state of Oregon.

Further help should come from the CFE cuts that are now shaping up. Under pressure to conclude CFE I in time to hold the planned CSCE summit in November and bless German unification, all the major powers agreed, in the two-plus-four talks, to set this fall as the target for signing the first conventional-arms-control treaty. Indications are that even the Russians will go ahead with CFE I, essentially on the strength of Bonn's pledge of a 370,000-man ceiling on future German armed forces.

If present trends continue, America's and NATO's main policy choices will concern shaping their forces for the 1990s in the most stabilizing way and setting goals for follow-on CFE negotiations.

The danger of crisis instability from panicky or automatic mobilization (as in the World War I scenario) will, of course, be more remote in a landscape in which East and West are not locked, as in the past, in permanent armored standoff on the Elbe and Werra rivers. And the greater relaxation of pulled-back forces will make it less urgent to react hastily to ambiguous warning signals. Moreover, budgetary constraints will preclude development of the more exotic and potentially destabilizing high-tech weapons for interdiction of second-echelon forces far behind enemy front lines.

Yet future forces will almost certainly be designed around the potentially destabilizing precepts of mobility and reliance on mobilization of reserves to enable fewer troops to defend more territory. Tactics are likely to follow the principles of maneuver warfare, in which a premium is put on preemption and creation of a fait accompli—and small changes in already reduced deployments could have a magnified significance.

Some bilateral and mutual restraints, therefore, must be thought through for the new era to avoid having one side's prudent defensive preparations misread by the other as offensive intent.

In the follow-on CFE negotiations, the United States and NATO should aim to diminish the threat of sustained, mobilized attack in the same way they aimed to diminish the threat of short-warning attack in CFE I. Further CFE agreements should also fill some of the large gaps left after CFE I and limit aircraft, bridge-building, and other logistical equipment for offensive operations; reduce Soviet troops in the European part of the Soviet Union west of the Urals and overall alliance (rather than just American and Soviet) military manpower; and restrict production of new tanks and other heavy weapons that might otherwise replace the materiel to be destroyed under CFE I.

Nuclear Issues

The one facet of transatlantic alliance that will require continued U.S. engagement in Europe well into the twenty-first century—even if present favorable trends continue—is nuclear deterrence. America's nuclear umbrella will still be needed to offset the Soviet nuclear arsenal that will continue to overshadow Europe. Barring unforeseen reversals in conventional arms cuts, though, it will no longer be needed to offset Soviet conventional superiority on the central front.

That is, America's "extended nuclear deterrence" will lose in practice its distinctive reservation of the right to resort to nuclear "first use" should any conventional Soviet attack begin defeating NATO forces. U.S. deterrence in Europe will thus become more analogous to U.S. strategic deterrence vis-à-vis the Soviet Union in envisaging firing nuclear missiles only in retaliation for any Soviet nuclear first strike.

The United States need not and should not institute any declaratory policy of no first use of nuclear weapons in Europe beyond the rhetorical demotion of nuclear warheads to "weapons of last resort" at the NATO summit in July 1990. Further nuclear de-emphasis will occur of its own accord as East-West relations improve, and a kind of residual deterrence is prudent so long as any risk of relapse to Soviet militarism remains.*

---

* See both Walter B. Slocombe, "Strategic Stability in a Restructured World,"

Nuclear peace has by now given Europe its longest period without war since the Middle Ages, and this achievement should be consolidated before the means that secured it are discarded.*

This accomplishment—along with the disappearance of the cold war need for nuclear arms control to carry the burden in East-West dealings normally borne by political relations—should make nuclear issues far less controversial in U.S.-German relations in the 1990s than they were in the 1980s. In this perspective, the dispute over INF deployments was probably the last abolitionist fight of the era that established nuclear peace in Europe as a given.

The present equilibrium could still revert to polarization within the Western alliance, however, if the United States is perceived as not exercising its nuclear stewardship responsibly and seeking to tame the monster by nuclear reductions. It therefore behooves the United States to make the necessary political push to conclude the Strategic Arms Reductions Treaty (START) along the broad lines of agreement that have been clear since 1988. Basically, this is a question of relations between the superpowers, of course, rather than of America's relations with Germany or Europe. It has such a fundamental bearing on West-West relations, though, that it must be considered in this context as well. After all the Soviet concessions in past START negotiations (and in Eastern Europe), Europeans in general and Germans in particular would tend to attribute any ultimate miscarriage of START to the United States.

At the moment, START is barely on the threshold of consciousness, either in Germany or in the United States. But an American failure to

---

and William D. Bajusz and Lisa D. Shaw, "The Forthcoming 'SNF Negotiations,' " in *Survival* 32, no. 4 (July/August 1990), pp. 299-312 and pp. 333-47, respectively. For discussion of NATO nuclear issues before November 1989, see both Hans Binnendijk, "NATO's Nuclear Modernization Dilemma," and Michael M. May, Paul T. Herman, and Sybil Francis, "Dealing with Nuclear Weapons in Europe," *Survival* 31, no. 2 (March/April 1989), pp. 137-55 and pp. 157-70, respectively.

* Here I accept the arguments of mainstream strategists that the prospect of nuclear holocaust is so horrifying that it has broken the habit of war in previously war-prone Europe, the locale of the most intense confrontation between the nuclear superpowers. See, e.g., Carl Kaysen, "Is War Obsolete? A Review Essay," *International Security* 14, no. 4 (Spring 1990), pp. 42-64, discussing John Mueller's *Retreat from Doomsday: The Obsolescence of Major War* (New York: Basic Books, 1989).

codify and sign superpower nuclear restraint in the present era of East-West rapprochement—when the fading Soviet threat no longer compels Western solidarity despite differences of outlook—could poison alliance relations. Kohl's government would no doubt accept American arguments that mutual superpower restraint could continue without written rules. But the first major crisis and war scare would revive all the popular German fears of the early 1980s about trigger-happy Americans.

Helpful, but less crucial in West-West relations, would be an American initiative that went beyond START I to propose cutting nuclear warheads to a few thousand for each superpower.

The specifics of America's nuclear umbrella for Europe is a more complex issue. For a quarter century, the United States has said, in the name of "flexible response," that it might well escalate to nuclear war in Europe if the Warsaw Treaty Organization attacked conventionally and NATO were losing the war. The reasoning was not only that NATO needed to compensate for Soviet superiority in heavy ground weapons on the central front, but also that conventional deterrence alone, even if NATO achieved parity with the Warsaw Treaty Organization, could not be trusted. Too often in history—as in 1939—it has failed to prevent the outbreak of war. The much more daunting nuclear deterrence has been needed to instill the proper inhibitions against starting any war.

Once the Soviet Union achieved rough strategic parity with the United States in the 1970s, however, the credibility of America's extended nuclear deterrence in Europe fell under increasing doubt, from two opposite directions. Numerous Europeans in the security establishments observed that NATO simulations began showing no Western advantage—and even considerable disadvantage—from nuclear escalation. They therefore asked if the United States would really be so irrational as to "sacrifice Chicago for Hamburg"—to retaliate for any Soviet seizure of a West German city with nuclear strikes on Ukrainian missile sites, when the Soviets would thereafter certainly fire a re-retaliatory strike on an American city. Obversely, the Germans began worrying that the U.S. nuclear commitment was all too credible and might drag Europe into a war that would raze it while somehow leaving the superpowers less scathed.

The suicidal threat of extended nuclear deterrence always was irrational—as were Khrushchev's explicit threats to incinerate Italian lemon groves during the Berlin crisis of the early 1960s, and Brezhnev's implicit claim to the same right, should NATO deploy its INF missiles, in the 1980s. But NATO nuclear deterrence, even of conventional war in Europe, always rested not on rationality, but on the 5 percent Soviet uncertainty, as it was often described, that the United States might in fact act irrationally in the heat of crisis. And this deterrence by uncertainty was remarkably sturdy, depending less on specific weapons and ranges than on that fear of emotional or even inadvertent escalation.

Now that sweetness and light have broken out between East and West, American deterrence is even less rational and more sturdy than it ever was. That 5 percent deterrence by uncertainty has become a 1 percent residual insurance against any relapse to Soviet militarism (or even acquisition of Soviet nuclear weapons by irresponsible national minorities, should civil war erupt in the Soviet Union). This reduced dependence on nuclear deterrence—along with the offer by the United States and NATO in summer 1990 to negotiate deep (or probably total) cuts in short-range ground-based nuclear weapons in Europe—precludes resumption of the once-burning dispute between Germany and the United States about upgrading NATO's 110-kilometer-range Lance missile. That strife is well gone; the United States (and Britain) were ill-advised to make that single weapon for a single "rung" of targets a free-floating test of German loyalty to the alliance.

Several unresolved nuclear issues do remain between the United States and Germany, however, including the number of nuclear warheads that will remain in Germany, their possible use in any "general nuclear response," and new stand-off missiles on aircraft.

All the allies agree that the present concentration of the bulk of NATO's four thousand tactical nuclear warheads on German soil is excessive. It will indeed be reduced as East and West negotiate down their remaining short-range systems in the next few years—and, in the process, new criteria will have to be worked out to determine equitable numbers of nuclear weapons to be deployed in Germany.

One rule in that determination must be that weapons with primary missions in a "general nuclear response"—that is, an all-out Soviet-American nuclear exchange—must no longer be stationed in Germany. Assignment of weapons in this category to Germany drove up deployment numbers in the past, and it evoked considerable bitterness among some German officials—though they never voiced this publicly—at what seemed to them to be disproportionate German risk for the sake of the United States.

Conversely, nuclear numbers in Germany should probably not drop to zero. Residual nuclear deterrence could, of course, be underwritten by American sea- and air-launched missiles without any land-based warheads in Germany. A totally nuclear-free Germany would, however, be opting out of NATO's nuclear risk sharing altogether, and would court the long-feared hazard of "decoupling" Germany from the United States. Under unfavorable conditions, Germans could come to doubt the "credibility" of the American nuclear umbrella if no U.S. nuclear weapons were present in Germany to guarantee America's immediate involvement in any hostilities. Under further unfavorable conditions, such a state could lead, not to nuclear pacifism, as in the 1980s, but to an eventual desire by the new Germany to acquire nuclear weapons to assure deterrence of war in Europe.

Such a development is unlikely. Until now, contrary to every expectation when the British and French first acquired their independent nuclear forces, the Germans have not wanted to have nuclear weapons of their own, and they look with dismay at any suggestion by American academics that they should go nuclear. Initially, this inferior status was forced on them by the World War II victors. By now, however, nuclear weapons have been shown to confer such negligible operational influence in Europe—beyond their all-important ban on any war—that the Germans are glad to invest their resources elsewhere.

Paradoxically, then, retention of some American nuclear weapons based in Germany in the 1990s should help ensure that a future Germany does not feel compelled to acquire nuclear weapons. And such retention would have the further advantage of maintaining the German voice in NATO nuclear decisions in continuing Germany's first-class membership in NATO's two nuclear steering committees of the Nuclear Planning Group and High Level Group.

If these hypotheses are correct and all ground-based nuclear missiles are removed from Germany in the early 1990s, prudence would suggest that NATO's forthcoming tactical air-to-surface missile—the one controversial weapon system still on the horizon—be based on aircraft stationed in Germany as well as in Britain and France. Currently, there is a moratorium on discussing this issue until after the German election in December 1990, but some alliance decisions will have to be made in the early 1990s.

Politically, refitting nuclear-capable planes with stand-off missiles has been much less controversial in Germany, so far, than deploying much more visible and totemic ground-launched missiles. Especially in the less-nuclear world now beginning, in which squadrons are being cut anyway and there is no war scare as there was in the early 1980s, it would seem possible to persuade the German public of the worth of the trade-off. If permanent basing of NATO aircraft capable of carrying nuclear stand-off weapons is not possible in Germany, then rotation of such aircraft in and out of German airfields should be possible.

In this regard, the whole East-West relaxation, the reassurance in the drawdown in Soviet conventional superiority, and the relief of knowing that no one is really going to use nuclear weapons in Europe all make it much easier to reach alliance compromises. The NATO military command has finally grasped that it cannot stage unrealistic "Wintex" and "Cimex" nuclear-war-game simulations in today's climate. Weapons planners are already drawing up fewer of their grisly, arcane scenarios; there are therefore fewer of the old insoluble clashes between U.S. strategists who want any theater nuclear response to avoid striking the Soviet Union in order to provide a "firebreak" for stopping the war and German strategists who want any theater nuclear response to strike the Soviet Union immediately to deliver the warning where it counts—and avoid the situation of "the shorter the range, the deader the Germans."

Afterword

From 1948 on, U.S. policy toward Germany was a function of super-power relations. Now, to a considerable extent, superpower relations have become a function of both Washington's and Moscow's policies toward Germany.

Put another way, German unification is a catalyst, for Europe and for East-West relations. First, it changed the entire role of strategic arms control, which from the late 1960s until 1989 was the fulcrum of East-West relations and a conscious surrogate for virtually nonexistent political relations. German unification effected, or at least consummated, the restoration of politics to superpower stage center, in a way that both Presidents Carter and Reagan tried, but failed, to do earlier.

Next, it gave urgency to West European integration and revived a dynamic the continent had lost a century earlier to the sub-European peripheries of the United States and then the Soviet Union. And finally, it defined with clarity the reentry of Eastern Europe to Europe proper, as well as the terms of entry to Europe for the Russian outsider.

In one sense, the United States has been a distant, lucky bystander to this historic drama. In another sense, the United States has magnified its benefit by its activist intervention on behalf of unification. It won German gratitude, and it helped preserve a viable NATO. There has been a synergy at work in Kohl's, Bush's, Genscher's, and Baker's application to the international scene of their honed sensitivities to domestic politics.

The precise "architecture" of the resulting post-cold-war system in Europe is hard to discern, not only because it has not yet emerged, but also because the multiplicity of overlapping institutions blurs the lines of responsibility. The simplicity of bipolar confrontation—NATO and the European Community on our side, the Warsaw Treaty Organization and the Council for Mutual Economic Assistance on theirs—is yielding to a much more nebulous arrangement.

The European Community, the core magnet which other institutions will increasingly orient themselves to, is holding itself open to association and probably eventual membership for East European nations that qualify economically and politically. It is further helping train them to achieve these qualifications, and it is coordinating Western financial aid to undergird the new democracies economically. It will also take the lead in the single most important service to the Central European economies in keeping Western markets open to their exports.

At the same time that it is looking to the East, the once purely economic European Community is encroaching more and more in the West on what used to be the sovereign policy prerogatives of its own members, and is declaring that "widening" its reach eastward must not prejudice the "deepening" of foreign policy coordination among them into "political union." This extension of the European Community's authority increasingly covers security policy, despite neutral Ireland.

The United States can watch these developments with equanimity. It does not have to sort out the difficult problems of redressing the "democratic deficit" of unifying Europeans, of balancing rival Sicilian and Galician claims to economic stimulation, of forcing farmers into a real market economy while still preserving village virtues. And it should not worry about European Community trespasses on NATO turf.

The European Community will probably resume political initiatives in the Middle East at some point and perhaps even assist in solving some aspect of that stalemate. Having so recently awakened from its decades of slumber in economic affairs, however, it is going to be fully occupied with 1992 and central banks and German unification and Britain's post-Thatcher resignation to European identity. The European Community will not be eager to take on the additional security burdens that NATO currently bears. And dual members of the European Community and NATO are unlikely to discard soon the advantages they derive from America's role in NATO as equalizer and occasional alibi in leadership.

Nor will CSCE, as it is now shaping up, be a rival for NATO. It will promote transparency and predictability in military affairs through negotiated East-West confidence-building and verification measures—and through eventually bringing the European neutrals too into CFE arms control. It will certainly provide in its peripatetic conferences a forum in which West Europeans can help steady developments in Central Europe. If pressed, it may even manage to field a peacekeeping force to help Hungarians and Romanians, or Albanians and Serbs, practice self-restraint in not shooting at each other—a task NATO could certainly not perform in the 1990s without agitating the Soviet Union. In northern Central Europe, CSCE might also sponsor military links between, say, Poland, Sweden, and Finland.

CSCE, reinforced by the Council of Europe, will further continue to set democratic standards for Central Europe as it did in the 1980s, this time less in individual human rights than in rule of law and tolerance of minorities and of pluralism. Again, this is a job that NATO could not do, but one that benefits the entire West by encouraging moderation and stability in Central Europe. The genius of CSCE is that, however haphazard the process by which it hammered together recognition of boundaries, human rights, economic cooperation, confidence-building measures, and environmental concern, these disparate elements now form a recognized whole, and have proven their mettle in the changes they have inspired in Eastern Europe and the Soviet Union.

Other European actors who will participate in less prominent ways in stabilizing the new Europe include the new European Bank for Reconstruction and Development, individual governments (which may give or underwrite credits, provide tax breaks for investors in Central Europe, or take such actions as setting up special economic zones on the German-Polish border), and European and especially German businessmen.

By contrast, the United States is mostly applauding the Europeans. Far from organizing any new Marshall Plan for Central Europe, it has abdicated leadership and has so far committed only a small $1 billion in loans and credits to the region. And American investors seem more interested in quick profits than in the long-term possibilities now opening up in Central Europe.

In the 1990s, the better part of valor in the German and European policies of a deficit America will perhaps be grace in leaving the lead in the metamorphosis to those Europeans who are directly involved.

*   *   *

In the present hangover from the rush to German unification, any analyst who is optimistic risks being judged frivolous for ignoring the grave dangers in the breakup of the old stability in Europe.

Certainly the dangers exist. Managing Soviet decline, German ascent, and Central European turmoil will not be easy. Preserving the congruence between democracy, prosperity, and peace will not be easy, especially in the wake of the Iraqi crisis, especially in light of swiftly rising expectations and pent-up nationalist animosities in Central Europe. The 1990s will test German—and American—maturity.

Yet there was more political movement in the single year of 1989-90 than in the four previous, frozen decades. There was astonishingly swift transformation in Central Europe. There was astonishing movement toward German unification, astonishing success of the West's subsequent ad hoc policy, astonishing consensus at the end of the day in the response of the major players, astonishing "stability" in this utter rupture of the previous, familiar system of peace and division. The partition of the continent, like the partition of Germany itself, has ended, peacefully. Central Europe is now returning to Europe. Russia may finally be entering Europe.

Surely in this transformation there is ground for optimism—and even awe.

Bibliography

Books

Albers, D., Frank Deppe, and Michael Stamm. *Fernaufklarung, Glasnost und die bundesdeutsche Linke.* Cologne: Klepenheuer and Witsch, 1989.

Arnold, Karl-Heinz, *Die ersten hundert Tage: Hans Modrow.* (East) Berlin: Dietz, 1990

Aslund, Anders. *Private Enterprise in Eastern Europe.* New York: St. Martin's Press, 1985.

Bark, Dennis L. and David Gress. *A History of West Germany, vol. 1 1945-1963, vol. 2 1963-1988.* Cambridge: Basil Blackwell, 1989.

Bender, Peter. *Deutsche Parallelen.* Berlin: Siedler, 1989.

_____. Bender, Peter. *Das Ende des Ideologischen Zeitalters. Die Europäisierung Europas.* Berlin: Severin und Siedler, 1981.

Blackwill, Robert D. and F. Stephen Larrabee. *Conventional Arms Control and East-West Security.* Durham: Duke University Press, 1989.

Blechman, Barry M. and Cathleen S. Fisher. *The Silent Partner: West Germany and Arms Control.* Cambridge: Ballinger, 1988.

Boutwell, Jeffrey. *The German Nuclear Dilemma.* Ithaca: Cornell University Press, 1990.

Bulmer, Simon and William Paterson. *The Federal Republic of Germany and the European Community.* London: Allen & Unwin, 1987.

Calingaert, Michael. *The 1992 Challenge from Europe.* Washington, D.C.: National Planning Association, 1989.

Calleo, David P. *Beyond American Hegemony: The Future of the Western Alliance.* New York: Basic, 1987.

Campbell, Edwina S. *Germany's Past and Europe's Future: The Challenges of West German Foreign Policy.* Washington, D.C.: Pergamon-Brassey's, 1989.

Childs, David. *The GDR: Moscow's German Ally.* Boston: Allen & Unwin, 1983.

Cimbala, Stephen J. *NATO Strategies and Nuclear Weapons.* New York: St. Martin's Press, 1989.

Clemens, Clay. *Reluctant Realists: the CDU/CSU and West German Ostpolitik, 1969-1982.* Durham: Duke University Press, 1989.

Colchester, Nicholas and David Buchan. *Europe Relaunches.* London: Hutchinson/Economist Books, 1990.

Cooney, James A., Wolfgang-Uwe Friedrich, and Gerald R. Kleinfeld, eds. *German-American Relations Yearbook 1.* Frankfurt/New York: Campus Verlag, 1989.

Craig, Gordon. *The Germans.* New York: G. P. Putnam's Sons, 1982.

Cuthbertson, Ian M. and David Robertson. *Enhancing European Security: Living in a Less Nuclear World.* New York: St. Martin's Press, 1990.

Dahrendorf, Ralf. *Society and Democracy in Germany.* Garden City: Anchor Books, 1969.

Dean, Jonathan. *Watershed in Europe: Dismantling the East-West Military Confrontation.* Lexington: Lexington Books, 1987.

_____. *Meeting Gorbachev's Challenge: How to Build Down the NATO-Warsaw Pact Confrontation.* New York: St. Martin's Press, 1989.

DePorte, A. W. *Europe between the Superpowers: The Enduring Balance.* New Haven: Yale University Press, 1986.

Evans, Richard J. *In Hitler's Shadow.* New York: Pantheon, 1989.

Flynn, Gregory, ed. *The West and the Soviet Union: Politics and Policy.* New York: St. Martin's Press, 1990.

Freedman, Lawrence. *Europe Transformed.* New York: St. Martin's Press, 1990.

_____. *The Evolution of Nuclear Strategy.* New York: St. Martin's Press, 1989.

Fritsch-Bournazel, Renata. *Confronting the German Question: Germans on the East-West Divide.* Oxford: Berg, 1988.

Gaddis, John Lewis. *Strategies of Containment.* Oxford: Oxford University Press, 1982.

_____. *The Long Peace: Inquiries into the History of the Cold War*. New York: Oxford University Press, 1987.

Garton Ash, Timothy. *The Uses of Adversity*. New York: Vintage, 1990.

_____. *The Magic Lantern*. New York: Random House, 1990.

Gati, Charles. *The Bloc That Failed*. Bloomington: Indiana University Press, 1990.

Gaus, Günter. *Deutscher Lastenausgleich*. Frankfurt: Luchterhand, 1990.

Gerster, Florian/Stobbe, Dietrich. *Die linke Mitte Heute*. Bonn: Dietz Nachf., 1990.

Gremliza, Hermann L. *Krautland einig Vaterland*. Hamburg: Konkret, 1990.

Griffith, William E. ed. *Central and Eastern Europe: The Opening Curtain?* Boulder: Westview, 1989.

Grosser, Alfred. *The Western Alliance: European-American Relations Since 1945*. New York: Continuum, 1980.

Habermas, Jürgen. *Die nachholende Revolution*. Frankfurt: Suhrkamp, 1990.

Hanrieder, Wolfram F. *Germany, America, Europe: Forty Years of German Foreign Policy*. New Haven: Yale University Press, 1989.

Hein, Christoph. *Die fünfte Grundrechenart: Aufsatze und Reden 1987- 1990*. Frankfurt: Luchterhand, 1990.

Heym, Stefan. *Einmischung: Gesprache, Reden, Essays*. Munich: Bertelsmann, 1990.

James, Harold A. *A German Identity 1770-1990*. New York: Routledge, 1990.

Joffe, Josef. *The Limited Partnership: Europe, the United States, and the Burdens of Alliance*. Cambridge: Ballinger, 1987.

Kaiser, Karl and Pierre Lellouche (Deutsche Gesellschaft fur Auswartige Politik and Institut Francais des Relations Internationales) eds. *Deutsch-Französische Sicherheitspolitik*. Bonn: Europa Union Verlag, 1986.

Katzenstein, Peter J., *Policy and Politics in West Germany: The Growth of a Semi-Sovereign State*. Philadephia: Temple University Press, 1987.

Kelleher, Catherine McArdle. *Germany and the Politics of Nuclear Weapons*. New York: Columbia University Press, 1975.

Kittrie, Nicholas N. and Ivan Volgyes. *Eastern Europe between the Superpowers: The Quest for a New Balance*. Washington, D.C.: Washington Institute Press, 1990.

Kommers, Donald P. *Constitutional Jurisprudence of the Federal Republic of Germany.* Durham: Duke University Press, 1989.

Krenz, Egon. *Wenn Mauern fallen.* Vienna: Neff, 1990.

Krisch, Henry. *The German Democratic Republic.* Boulder: Westview, 1985.

Larrabee, F. Stephen, ed. *The Two German States and European Security.* New York: St. Martin's Press, 1989.

Maier, Charles S. *The Unmasterable Past: History, Holocaust, and German National Identity.* Cambridge: Harvard Unviersity Press, 1988.

Marsh, David. *The Germans: Rich, Bothered and Divided.* London: Century, 1989.

McAdams, A. James. *East Germany and Detente.* New York: Cambridge University Press, 1985.

Merkl, Peter H., ed. *The Federal Republic of Germany at Forty.* New York: New York University Press, 1989.

Moreton, Edwina, ed. *Germany between East and West.* Cambridge: Cambridge University Press, 1987.

Müller, Heiner. *Zur Lage der Nation, Interview mit Frank M. Raddatz.* Berlin: Rotbuch, 1990.

Nawrocki, Joachim. *Relations between the Two States in Germany.* Bonn: The Press and Information Office of the Federal Government, undated—available 1990.

Nelson, Daniel J. *Defenders or Intruders? The Dilemmas of U.S. Forces in Germany.* Boulder: Westview, 1987.

Neues Forum Leipzig. eds. *Jetzt oder Nie-Demokratie: Leipziger Herbst '89.* Munich: Bertelsmann, 1990.

Rein, Gerhard, ed. *Die Opposition in der DDR.* Berlin: Wicheren, 1990.

Rueschemeyer, Marilyn and Christiane Lemke. *The Quality of Life in the German Democratic Republic.* Armonk, New York: M.E. Sharpe, 1989.

Schmidt, Helmut. *Men and Powers: A Political Retrospective.* New York: Random House, 1990.

Schulz, Eberhard. *Die deutsche Frage und die Nachbarn im Osten.* Munich: R. Oldenbourg, 1989.

Schwarz, Hans-Peter. *Die gezähmten Deutschen. Von der Machtbesessenheit zur Machtsvergessenheit.* Stuttgart: Deutsche Verlags-Anstalt, 1985.

Schweigler, Gehard. *Grundlagen der aussenpolitischen Orientierung der Bundesrepublik.* Baden-Baden: Nomos, 1985.

Simons, Thomas W., Jr. *The End of the Cold War?* New York: St. Martin's Press, 1990.

Sloan, Stanley. *NATO in the 1990s.* Washington, D.C.: Pergamon-Brassey's, 1989.

Smyzer, William R. *Restive Partners—Washington and Bonn Diverge.* Boulder: Westview Press, 1990.

Stromseth, Jane E. *The Origins of Flexible Response: NATO's Debate Over Strategy in the 1960s.* New York: St. Martin's Press, 1988.

Turner, Henry Ashby, Jr. *The Two Germanies since 1945.* New Haven: Yale University Press, 1987.

Weidenfeld, Werner. ed. *Geschichtsbewusstsein der Deutschen.* Cologne: Verlag Wissenschaft und Politik (second edition), 1989.

Weidenfeld, Werner and Zimmermann, Hartmut, eds. *Deutschland-Handbuch.* Bonn: Bundeszentrale fur politische Bildung, 1989.

Wells, Samuel, Jr., ed. *The Helsinki Process and the Future of Europe.* Washington: The Wilson Center Press, 1990.

West German Foreign Ministry. *Umbruch in Europa: Die Ereignisse im 2. Halbjahr 1989.* Bonn: Foreign Ministry of the Federal Republic of Germany, 1990.

Current Articles

Barnet, Richard. "Defining the Moment." *The New Yorker,* July 16, 1990, pp. 46-53.

Brzezinski, Zbigniew. "Beyond Chaos: A Policy for the West." *The National Interest,* Spring 1990, pp. 3-12.

_____. "Post-Communist Nationalism." *Foreign Affairs* 68, no. 5 (Winter 1989/90), pp. 1-25.

Dahrendorf, Ralf (interview). "Threats to Civil Society, East and West." *Harper's,* July 1990, pp. 24-32.

Dean, Jonathan. "Components of a Post-Cold War Security System for Europe." Working Paper at Ninth Workshop of the Pugwash Study Group on "Conventional Forces in Europe," April 17-21, 1990, Vienna, Austria.

_____. "Building a Post-Cold War European Security System." *Arms Control Today,* June 1990, pp. 8-12.

Garton Ash, Timothy. "The Chequers Affair." *New York Review of Books*, September 27, 1990, p. 65.

_____. "Eastern Europe: Après le Déluge, Nous." *New York Review of Books*, August 16, 1990, pp. 51-57.

Gedmin, Jeffrey. "East Germany's Disappearing Future." *Problems of Communism*, March-April 1990, pp. 85-114.

Howorth, Jolyon. "France since the Berlin Wall: Defence and Diplomacy." *The World Today*, July 1990, pp. 126-30.

Keithly, David M. "The German Fatherland—of the Left." *Orbis*, Winter 1990, pp. 67-82.

Kennan, George F. "This Is No Time to Talk of German Reunification." *Washington Post*, November 12, 1990, p. D1.

Latey, Maurice. "Germany I: Two Cheers for Democracy." *The World Today*, May 1990, pp. 77-78.

Lisiecki, Jerry. "Financial and Material Transfers Between East and West Germany." *Soviet Studies* 42, no. 3, July 1990, pp. 513-34.

Mearsheimer, John. "Why We Will Soon Miss the Cold War." *Atlantic*, August 1990, pp. 35-50.

Mielke, Erich and other East German secret-police officials. "Ich liebe euch doch alle…" *Befehle und Lageberichte des MfS, January-November 1989.* (East) Berlin: BasisDruck, 1990.

Newhouse, John. "Sweeping Change." *The New Yorker*, August 27, 1990, pp. 78-89.

Pond, Elizabeth. "A Wall Destroyed: The Dynamics of German Unification in the GDR." *International Security* 15, no. 2 (Fall 1990), pp. 35-66.

Roper, John. "Europe and the Future of Germany—A British View." *The World Today*, March 1990, pp. 46-49.

Schirrmacher, Frank. "Jeder Is mit Seiner Wahrheit Allein." *Frankfurter Allgemeine Zeitung*, April 10, 1990, first page of literature section.

Snyder, Jack. "Averting Anarchy in the New Europe." *International Security* 14, no. 4 (Spring 1990), pp. 5-41.

Wallace, William and Säpt, Martin. "Coming to Terms with Germany." *The World Today*, April 1990, pp. 55-56.

Wat, Donald Cameron. "Germany II: The Case against Bourbonism." *The World Today*, May 1990, pp. 79-82.

Articles, Earlier Material

Asmus, Ronald D. "Bonn and East Berlin: The 'New' German Question?" *The Washington Quarterly* 9, no. 1 (Winter 1986), pp. 47-66.

Bender. Peter. "The Superpower Squeeze." *Foreign Policy* (Winter 1986/87), pp. 98-106.

Clemens, Clay. "Beyond INF: West Germany's Centre-Right Party and Arms Control in the 1990s." *International Affairs,* Winter 1988/89, pp. 55-74.

Dudney, Robert S. "New Fissures in NATO." *Air Force Magazine,* October 1988, pp. 34-40.

Fitzsimons, Alastair. "Current European Institutional Approaches to Security." *International Defense Review,* April 1989, pp. 409-10.

Friedrich, Wolfgang-Uwe. "The German Question between West and East." *Aussenpolitik* (English), March 1987, pp. 242-57.

Hampson, Fen Osler. "NATO Fissures." *Peace and Security* (Canada) 3, no. 2 (Summer 1988), pp. 10-11.

Katzenstein, Peter J. "The Third West German Republic: Continuity in Change." *Journal of International Affairs* 41, no. 2 (Summer 1988), pp. 325-44.

MacGregor, Douglas A. "Force Development in the Warsaw Pact: The Soviet-East German Connection." *Armed Forces and Society* 14, no. 4 (Summer 1988), pp. 527-48.

Löwenthal, Richard. "The Federal Republic: An Integral Part of the Western World." *German Issues* 2, Washington, D.C.: American Institute of Contemporary German Studies, June 1986.

McAdams, A. James. "The New Logic in Soviet-GDR Relations." *Problems of Communism,* September-October 1988, pp. 47-60.

Mushaben, Joyce Marie. "A Search for Identity: The 'German Question' in Atlantic Alliance Relations." *World Politics* 40, no. 3 (April 1988), pp. 395-417.

Pond, Elizabeth. "Andropov, Kohl, and East-West Issues." *Problems of Communism* 32, no. 4 (July-August 1983), pp. 35-45.

Schneider, Peter. "Is There A Europe?" *Harper's* 277, no. 1660 (September 1988), pp. 55-59.

Schweigler, Gebhard L. "Anti-Americanism in Germany." *The Washington Quarterly* 9, no. 1 (Winter 1986), pp. 67-84.

Scruton, Roger. "Don't Trust the Germans." *Sunday Telegraph,* May 21, 1989.

Stürmer, Michael. "Making Sense of Deutschlandpolitik." *The Washington Quarterly* 9, no. 1 (Winter 1986), pp. 85-92.

Thies, Jochen. "West Germany: The Risks Ahead." *The World Today*, May 1989, pp. 76-79.

Tismaneanu, Vladimir. "Nascent Civil Society in the German Democratic Republic." *Problems of Communism*, March-June 1989, pp. 88-111.

Treverton, Gregory. "Europe-Bashing in U.S. Domestic Politics." *Peace and Security* 3, no. 3 (Autumn 1988), pp. 6-7.

Papers, Speeches, Interviews

Bush, George and Baker, James. Speeches, distributed by The White House and State Department press offices.

Gorbachev, Mikhail, and Shevardnadze, Eduard. Speeches and interviews, as translated in the Federal Broadcast Information Service in Washington, D.C., including especially Eduard Shevardnadze (interview), "On Foreign Policy," *Pravda*, June 26, 1990, translation in Federal Broadcast Information Service, Washington, D.C.

Hamilton, Daniel. "After the Revolution." German Issues #7. Washington, D.C.: American Institute for Contemporary German Studies, The Johns Hopkins University Press, April 1990.

Kennan, George F. "The German Problem: A Personal View." Washington, D.C.: The American Institute for Contemporary German Studies, The Johns Hopkins University Press, April 1989.

Kohl, Helmut, and Genscher, Hans-Dietrich. Speeches, distributed by the West German Federal Press Office.

Mandelbaum, Michael. "Reconstructing the European Security Order," *Critical Issues 1990/1*. New York: Council on Foreign Relations, 1990.

Woodrow Wilson Center for Scholars, Series of Occasional Papers in 1990, "Beyond the Cold War: Current Issues in European Security," including Stephen Szabo, "The New Germany and European Security"; Lynn E. Davis, "Beyond German Unification: Defining the West's Strategic and Arms Control Policies"; Jenonne Walker, "Security in Post-Confrontation Europe"; and Lawrence Kaplan, "The End of the Alliance: Lessons of the 1960s."

Newspapers and Magazines

Running coverage from November 1, 1989, through September 8, 1990, in *Foreign Affairs, Deutschland Archiv, Der Spiegel, Die Zeit, Kirche im*

Sozialismus, the *Frankfurter Allegemeine Zeitung*, *Neues Deutschland*, the *Suddeutsche Zeitung*, *Tageszeitung*, *Die Welt*, the *Financial Times*, the *International Herald Tribune*, and the *Economist*, including especially:

Asmus, Ronald D. "A United Germany," *Foreign Affairs* 69, no. 2 (Spring 1990), pp. 63-76.

Bertram, Christoph. "The German Question." *Foreign Affairs* 69, no. 2 (Spring 1990), pp. 45-62.

Betz, Hans-Georg. "Strange Love? How the Greens Began to Love NATO," *German Studies Review* 12, no. 3 (October 1989), pp. 487-505.

Bruce, Leigh. "Europe's Locomotive." *Foreign Policy* 78 (Spring 1990), pp. 68-90.

Dahrendorf, Ralf. "Transitions: Politics, Economics, and Liberty," *The Washington Quarterly* 13, no. 3 (Summer 1990), pp. 133-142.

"Eastern Europe . . . Central Europe . . . Europe." *Daedalus* 119, no. 1 (Winter 1990), discussions.

Garton Ash, Timothy. "Eastern Europe: The Fear of Truth," *New York Review of Books*, February 15, 1990, p. 17-22.

German Politics and Society, Issue 20 (Summer 1990) entire issue on "Germany: From Plural to Singular."

Gunlicks, Arthur B. "Federalism and Intergovernmental Relations in West Germany: A Fortieth Year Appraisal." *Publius* 19 (Fall 1989), pp. 17-238.

Hoagland, Jim. "Europe's Destiny." *Foreign Affairs* 69, no. 1 (America and the World 1989/90), pp. 33-50.

Howard, Michael. "The Springtime of Nations." *Foreign Affairs* 69, no. 1 (America and the World 1989/90), pp. 17-32.

Joffe, Josef. "Once More the German Question," *Survival* 32, no. 2 (March/April 1990), pp. 129-40.

Layne, Christopher. "Superpower Disengagement." *Foreign Policy* 77 (Winter 1989-90), pp. 17-40.

Maynes, Charles William. "America without the Cold War," *Foreign Policy* 78 (Spring 1990), pp. 3-25.

McAdams, A. James. "An Obituary for the Berlin Wall," *World Policy Journal* 7, no. 2 (Spring 1990), pp. 357-75.

Mearsheimer, John J., "Back to the Future: Instability in Europe after the Cold War," *International Security* 15, no. 1 (Summer 1990), pp. 5-56.

Moïsi, Dominique. "The French Answer to the German Question." *European Affairs,* Spring 1990.

Mueller, John. "A New Concept of Europe." *Foreign Policy* 77 (Winter 1989-90), pp. 3-16.

Nitze, Paul H. "America: An Honest Broker." *Foreign Affairs* 69, no. 4 (Fall 1990), pp. 1-14, plus five other articles on "A World Transformed." pp. 92-175.

Schneider, Peter. "Was wäre, wenn die Mauer fällt." *Tageszeitung,* November 14, 1989.

_____. "When the Two Germanys Unite, What Happens to the Bavarian Yodeler?" *New York Times Magazine,* September 16, 1990, pp. 41-108.

Schopflin, George. "Why Communism Collapsed." *International Affairs* 66, no. 1, pp. 3-16.

Seebacher-Brandt, Brigitte. "Die Linke und die Einheit." *Frankfurter Allegemeine Zeitung,* November 21, 1989.

Surveys: "On the Eve: A Survey of West Germany," *Economist,* October 28, 1989, and "The New Germany," *Economist,* June 30, 1990.

Svec, Milan. "East European Divides." *Foreign Policy* 77 (Winter 1989-90), pp. 41-63.

Szabo, Stephen F. "The German Answer." *SAIS Review,* 10, no. 2 (Summer/Fall 1990), pp. 41-56.

Tarnoff, Peter. "America's New Special Relationships." *Foreign Affairs* 69, no. 3 (Summer 1990), pp. 67-80.

Newhouse, John. "Sweeping Change." *The New Yorker,* August 27, 1990, pp. 78-89.

Von Staden, Berndt, "Nothing Less than the Whole of Europe Will Do . . ." *Aussenpolitik* (English) 41, no. 1, pp. 24-37.

Weilemann, Peter R. "The German Contribution toward Overcoming the Division of Europe—Chancellor Helmut Kohl's 10 Points." *Aussenpolitik* (English) 41, no. 1, pp. 15-23.

Wettig, Gerhard, "The German Problem in Soviet Policy." *Aussenpolitik* (English) 41, no. 1, pp. 38-51.

Index

Acheson, Dean, 1
Adenauer, Konrad, 19, 35, 36
Arms control, 3-4, 48-49, 50, 53, 64-65, 79, 82, 83, 85, 94-95. *See also* Nuclear arms control
Army (American): in Western Europe, 1, 62-63, 69, 73-74; in West Germany, 41, 42-43, 51, 64, 66, 72, 76, 77
Army (Eastern European), 49, 84, 95
Army (East German), 63, 66, 85
Army (Soviet), 86; in Eastern Europe, 2, 3, 4, 5, 26, 47; in East Germany, 10, 13, 14, 44, 51, 53, 64, 65, 66
Army (united Germany), 48, 63, 65-66, 73, 79, 81, 85
Army (Western European), 66, 81
Army (West German), 63-64, 66, 81-82, 85
Attitudes: British, 58; French, 25; German, 8-9, 10, 58, 79, 81-82; Western European, 78. *See also* Public opinion

Bad Godesberg program, 35
Bahr, Egon, 37, 42
Baker, James, 26-27, 31, 45
Balance of power, 1, 5, 25, 73, 82-83
Berlin Wall, 7-8, 10, 19, 39, 64, 83, 84, 88
Bohley, Bärbel, 11, 13, 19, 61
Böhme, Ibrahim, 58
Border: East-West German, 7, 11, 18, 65, 85; European, 52; German-Polish, 24, 55-58, 64, 65

Brandt, Willy, 9, 23, 35-36, 37, 38, 58
Brecht, Bertolt, 61
Bretton Woods agreement, 2
Brezhnev, Leonid, 49, 88
Brezhnev doctrine, 4
Brzezinski, Zbigniew, 73
Bulgaria, 4
Bundeswehr. *See* Army (West German)
Bureaucracy, 72, 81; French, 25; East German, 15, 16, 60
Bush, George, 26-27, 44-45, 56, 62-63, 71-72, 73-74
Bush administration, 67, 68, 71

Carter administration, 26, 71, 79, 93
CDU. *See* Christian Democratic Union
Censorship, 12, 37
Central bank: European, 22, 25, 94, 95; German, 33
Central Europe, 94, 95, 96
CFE. *See* Conventional forces in Europe
Christian Democratic Union (CDU: East Germany), 13, 18, 58, 59, 62
Christian Democratic Union (CDU: West Germany), 23, 38, 55-56
Christianity and politics, 10, 11, 12, 13, 30
Christian Social Union, 55
Citizens' committees, 23, 29, 30
Cold war, 9, 21, 57, 82
Collective security, 43, 53, 73, 81-82
Communism: in Eastern Europe, 3, 4, 19; in East Germany, 13, 62
Communist parties, 3, 4, 9, 15

INDEX   111

DUE DATE

DEC 1 5 2004

DEC 2 1 1992

JUL 0 2 1993

NOV 0 4 1993

JUL 0 5 1999

JUL 2 0 1999

FEB 0 7 2004